Social Anxiety Disorder

The Ultimate Practical Solutions to Overcoming Anxiety, Panic Attacks, Depression and Shyness Once and for All

Table of Contents

Chapter 1: Introduction 3

Chapter 2: Understanding Social Anxiety Disorder 5

Chapter 3: Overcoming Social Anxiety Disorder 17

Chapter 4: Mindfulness And Relaxation Techniques 74

Chapter 5: Improving Social Skills 106

Chapter 6: Conclusion 190

Chapter 1: Introduction

While the term "social anxiety" is often used nowadays, we have all overlooked the fact that this is a mental disorder (hence the name), and that it needs to be addressed. Of course, the word social anxiety disorder itself means that whoever has it is abnormal. The reality is that we all feel socially anxious at certain points in our lives. Social anxiety is a term used to describe a high level of shyness. We all feel shy or anxious in a certain social environment, especially if it is our first time being there. However, some people have it a little more extreme. When that is the case, it can have debilitating power in their lives and prevent them from doing the things they want to do.

For instance, it might prevent them from going to college or work because they are not confident. They might even be afraid to make friends and enjoy their hobbies. Most of the time, they over think that others will notice their social awkwardness and judge them negatively. Most of the time, socially anxious people feel that they are always under the spotlight and that everyone is thinking badly of them, even for the little things. They believe, quite firmly, that they are no good socially, and quite boring because they believe they have nothing interesting to bring to the table. After any social events, they often think back about it and pick out parts that they believe went poorly for them and beat themselves up over that.

If that sounds a lot like you or someone you know, then fret not. Social anxiety is not permanent, meaning that you can overcome it and become more successful in your life. This book will give you a better understanding of social anxiety disorder as well as providing practical tips to help you overcome this issue.

Chapter 2: Understanding Social Anxiety Disorder

To cope with social anxiety, many people often avoid social situations altogether if possible. If not, they try to stay in the background and attract as little attention to themselves as possible. Worse still, in more severe cases, people with social anxiety may not leave their house at all. But those are not all symptoms of social anxiety. If a number of the following applies to you, then you may be experiencing symptoms of social anxiety:

You feel on edge, anxious, vulnerable, under the spotlight, self-conscious, out of place, or embarrassed.

Your face goes red; you feel butterflies in your stomach or your stomach churns. Your heart races, your voice becomes shaky, your body trembles. You sweat, become dizzy or light-headed, and you breathe are shallow.

You might think that you have nothing interesting to say and think that you are boring. You might feel that everyone is staring at you in a disapproving manner. You imagine that people can tell at a glance how anxious you are. You think that you will stammer or blush. You tell yourself that you must not appear anxious. You think that you look and sound silly.

You tend to avoid social situations as much as possible. You tend to leave one as soon as you can. If not, you may stay in the background or hide, so to attract as little attention as possible. You tend to stay quiet out of fear that you may look and sound silly. You always go somewhere with your friend. Alcohol, to you, gives you courage before you mingle.

Now, if any of the above applies to you, there is no need to be alarmed as these behaviors are very common and there are plenty of things you can do to alleviate social anxiety. So, what causes social anxiety?

Theories

A theory suggests that we become socially anxious because of our past experience. For instance, if an infant touched a kettle and got severely burned from it, they will grow up thinking that kettle is a dangerous object and should be avoided in the future. The same applies to social anxiety. If someone felt embarrassed or humiliated in a past social situation, they might think that similar situations will go the same way in the future, and they are not willing to risk it ever again. They begin to fear that social situation as a result and avoid them.

Another theory suggests that some people think in a way that leads themselves to develop social anxiety. For instance, socially anxious people tend to think that they will perform poorly in a social situation. They think that everyone is paying attention to then, scrutinizing whatever they do or say, and then blame them for anything that they got wrong. They may also hold negative beliefs about their ability in a social situation. For example, they might think that they are boring and have nothing to contribute to the conversation. Of course, this way of thinking only leads to higher levels of social anxiety.

It is also possible that we develop social anxiety because of evolutionary factors. Think about it. We, humans, are social creatures, and we thrive in the company of others. As such, it makes a lot of sense that we prefer to avoid upsetting others and be rejected later on. Therefore, it is plausible that socially anxious individuals are just oversensitive to being negatively evaluated because of the disadvantages associated with it. This could explain why socially anxious people try their best not to offend others.

It is also possible that social anxiety has familial ties. For example, if someone in your family is socially anxious, chances are that someone else in the family is also socially anxious, or have similar personality traits. The chances are actually very high. Therefore, you can say that our genetics also play a huge role in the level of social anxiety we experience.

The reality is that you can be socially anxious because of a combination of these factors. However, it is less important to know what causes social anxiety. What is important is how to overcome it. But doing so is easier said than done. So, what stops us from overcoming or social anxiety?

Unhelpful Thoughts

Most of the time, people think unhelpful thoughts and predictions, making it much more difficult for them to overcome social anxiety. As mentioned previously, socially anxious people often have negative thoughts about themselves and their ability to socialize in social situations. This lowers their confidence and makes it more difficult to become engaged in a social situation. Therefore, they effectively ruin their chance of testing out their social skills and prove that they can actually interact well.

Moreover, unhelpful thoughts also play a damaging role just before people enter social environments because they predict they will do badly. They influence people during social situations because they think that they are not coming across well. To make things worse, after any social interaction, they often analyze their performance and conclude that they performed poorly. Considering all of these factors, it is not hard to see how unhelpful thoughts can stop people from overcoming social anxiety.

Avoidance

As previously mentioned, socially anxious individuals often avoid social contact whenever they can. If they cannot avoid it, they try to disengage as soon as possible. Though it may seem to be an effective way to cope with social anxiety, it is actually one of the reasons why people cannot overcome social anxiety.

When people avoid social situations, they stop themselves from having a positive experience that could debunk their negative beliefs. Moreover, the longer people avoid social situations, the more daunting and difficult to face they become.

Using "Safety Behaviors"

Most of the time, the only time when socially anxious individuals feel comfortable in social settings is when they employ what we call as "safety behavior". Such behaviors include trying to stay in the background as often as possible, remaining quiet during group conversations, sticking close to the person they know well, avoiding eye contact or drinking alcohol for more confidence. Basically, safety behavior is anything people do to allow them to cope in social situations better.

Although this sort of behaviors helps them feel better at the time, they are actually proving to be very unhelpful in the long run. Basically, this is hardly any different from avoidance. Such behaviors stop people from having the opportunity to prove that they can cope well without using these unnecessary precautions in the first place. What safety behaviors accomplish is offsetting success to other factors. For example, a socially anxious individual may attribute their socially successful evening to their friends, while it was actually them who performed well. Similarly, by remaining silent during conversations, they would not know if they would have coped well had they became more involved. As a result, their confidence remains low and their social anxiety lingers.

It is also worth noting that safety behaviors can lead to what is known as "self-fulling prophecies". For instance, by remaining silent during conversations, they might come across as "distant" and others may respond by making less of an effort if they continue to converse with the socially anxious at all. As a result, this further reinforces the beliefs of socially anxious individuals that they do not perform well without knowing that it is actually their "safety behaviors" that are damaging their social interactions.

Increased Self-Focus

Socially anxious individuals often spend a lot of time concentrating on their own bodily sensations during social interactions. This is a lot different from being mindful or being "present" at the moment. This self-focus also plays a part in keeping social anxiety going. For instance, people often spend time trying to judge whether they are stammering, shaking, blushing, or swearing during social situations. While they do this to monitor themselves so they can tell whether they are noticeable anxious, this can actually make thing a lot worse. When you start to monitor even those little things, you become very conscious of them, which makes us overestimate how visible our anxiety is and make us feel even more self-conscious. Moreover, when you focus on yourself, you do not fully focus on the conversation, making it harder for you to join in properly and therefore strengthens your belief that you are not good in such situations.

As always, social anxiety most likely comes from a combination of these factors.

Anxiety Attacks

An anxiety attack is a high-degree stress response that is activated when we are faced with an overly apprehensive behavior such as worrying or fearing something bad might happen, or when our body responds involuntarily to an abnormally high level of stress. In short, anxiety attacks have two main causes – voluntary and involuntary anxiety attacks. When we worry about something too much, and our body responds to the high level of stress, it is a voluntary anxiety attack. When our body activates a high-degree stress response because we are overly stressed for too long, it is an involuntary anxiety attack.

Voluntary Anxiety Attacks

Most anxiety attacks are voluntary because of overly apprehensive behaviors such as believing that something really bad is going to happen, which triggers our body to activate a high-degree stress response. When that happens, our physiological, psychological, and emotional states are changed drastically. While those changes are intended to help us in dangerous situations, they make us think that something really bad is happening, which cause us to worry more, which make us more stressed, and the cycle repeats. Therefore, reacting to anxiety attacks in a fearful way is similar to trying to put out the flame with gasoline.

In a way, anxious individuals become afraid of what the stress response feels like or think that it is something dangerous, which only causes them to be more stressed. This is often the condition that triggers the panic attack disorder. This is basically feeling afraid of the emotions or responses of high-degree stress response and thinking that it is something that cannot be controlled.

Here, fear sets off the first anxiety attack and the fear associated with the anxiety attack triggers more stress response. This is what we call the fear cycle. Voluntary anxiety attacks account for almost all of all anxiety attacks.

Involuntary Anxiety Attacks

Our body has a number of systems that automatically or involuntarily monitor and regulate each other every single second. When we are healthy and stress-free, all systems are working as intended. However, when we become stressed, things can kick into overdrive and some systems mismanage others, which can cause us to behave erratically and more involuntarily than normal. This behavior can cause our body to activate the stress response, which is responsible for most of the sudden and spontaneous anxiety attacks.

Chapter 3: Overcoming Social Anxiety Disorder

Thankfully, there are plenty of ways to reduce social anxiety. These strategies include:

- Learning how to challenge unhelpful thoughts and see things realistically
- Reduce the tendency of focusing on oneself during social interactions
- Removing the use of avoidance and safety behaviors and confronting fears gradually

It can be more helpful to try out these ideas one at a time rather than all of them at once. Simply take things at your own pace.

Challenging Unhelpful Thoughts

How we think about things have a huge impact on our social anxiety. Most of these thoughts occur outside our control and can be very damaging. Therefore, it is critical to remember that they are just thoughts without any real basis, and not facts. While we may believe most of our unhelpful thoughts when we are socially anxious, it is crucial to remember that your feelings should be questioned because most of them are based on invalid assumptions.

There are a few things you can do to help you begin to recognize if you are thinking in an unhelpful or unrealistic way and discuss how you can start to change this. When you do so, you can see things realistically, which help you overcome your social anxiety.

First, identify unhelpful thoughts about everything as they appear. They should be something like this:

Before social interactions:	During social interactions:	After social interactions:	About yourself:
I'll stammer/go bright red I'll have nothing worthwhile to say I'll make a fool of myself	I'm useless/trembling Everyone's staring at me They don't look like they agree with me	I shouldn't even bother in the first place I botched it Everyone thought I was an idiot	I'm unfunny Everyone hates me No one likes me

It can be hard to identify unhelpful thoughts, so try to think of the time when you are socially anxious. What went through your mind back then? Those might be unhelpful thoughts. You need to be able to identify unhelpful thoughts before you can challenge them. Recognizing common patterns that unhelpful thought follow can help you identify when you have them. There are a few common patterns to look out for:

Predicting the Future

When we feel shy or anxious, we often spend a lot of time thinking of what could go wrong in our next interaction rather than just let the small things slides. In the end, what we worry about the most did not happen and we ended up wasting time and energy being worried and upset about them. For instance, you might worry that you will go red, stammer, and everyone would dislike you. You might assume that you will be the center of attention and everyone will stare at you. Such thoughts only make you anxious before you even engage in social interaction.

Mind Reading

Basically, you make assumptions about others' beliefs without having any real evidence to support them. For example, you may think that the other person dislikes you, without actually knowing if they really do. Such a way of thinking can lower your mood and self-esteem.

Taking Things Personally

When you are shy or socially anxious, you would take things to heart often. For instance, just because your colleague is quiet does not mean that you have offended them and it is your fault. Just because a group is laughing as you walk by does not mean that the joke is aimed at you.

Overgeneralizing

You assume that all other incidents will follow a similar pattern just because of one isolated incident. For instance, you assume that all of your other presentations will be bad just because one went bad.

What-If Statements

Sometimes, we wonder "what if" things go wrong. Like, what if nobody likes us or what if we run out of things to say in the middle of the presentation? These thoughts often make you dread situations even before it happens.

Focusing on the Negatives

After any social gathering, you might focus on the parts of the evening that you think did not go well, while overlooking all the positive parts of the occasion. For instance, you might dwell on that one conversation that went bad quickly, while forgetting the fact that you have mingled well throughout the rest of the evening.

Labeling

Sometimes, you burden yourself with negative labels. You might think that you are boring, uninteresting, weird, or unlovable. These things are often long-held beliefs about yourself, which keep your confidence and self-esteem low.

Challenging Unhelpful Thoughts

From there, you need to make a list of unhelpful thoughts and categorize them so you know exactly what you did. From there, you can start to challenge your unhelpful thoughts by asking a few questions. For example, you are supposed to meet your friend's colleagues very soon, and you feel on edge or self-conscious. Your unhelpful thoughts are something like "I'll have nothing to say and they'll think I'm an idiot…" So, what can you do to challenge such thoughts? You can ask yourself a series of questions. Here are some examples of questions and answers:

- "Is there any evidence that contradicts this thought?" You should ask yourself this question first as it directly challenges the negative thought. Maybe you coped well when you were introduced to your brother's new partner or perhaps you rarely run out of things to say to your friends, so meeting your friend's colleagues should not be any different either.

- "Can I identify any of the patterns of unhelpful thinking described earlier?" In this case, you are predicting the future. You imagine that things will go badly for you, but the reality is that you cannot say for sure how it will go at all.
- "What would my friends say to me if they knew what I was thinking?" Most of the time, you are most likely thinking too much. Your friend would probably say something like "Don't be silly. You're always good company."
- "How will I feel about this in 6 months?" This helps put whatever you are worried about into perspective, especially if you are worrying too much. You most likely won't even care about it in six months, even if

things go wrong. You will have forgotten about it by then.

- "What are the costs and benefits of thinking in this way?" This question helps you understand just how damaging unhelpful thoughts can be. They will only make you nervous before you even go into the situation. The benefits? There are none.
- "Is there another way of looking at this situation?" Challenge yourself to see things differently if you want to overcome your social anxiety. In our example, suppose that you don't have anything to say, you should not worry still because it is not up to you alone to keep the conversation going. It is everyone's responsibility, so what do you really have to worry about?

When you have answered all of these questions, you should read through your answers and come up with a more balanced or rational view. For instance, instead of thinking "I'll have nothing to say and they'll think I'm an idiot…" say, "I cannot say for sure how it will go, but I know that I coped fine last week in a similar situation. So, hopefully, this will be the same. Then again, even if things don't go great, it's not the end of the world." It can help reduce your social anxiety if you apply these questions to the unhelpful thoughts that crop up. Reframe these negative thoughts into something that is realistic and balanced.

Reducing Internal Focus

We already talked about this, but when we are socially anxious, we often spend a lot of time concentrating on our own bodily sensations during social interactions. We are afraid that our anxiety will become visible to others. We do this to also reassure us that we are not visible anxious, which you can argue that it helps to cope with social anxiety, but the truth is that it prevents you from fully concentrating on the conversation, therefore actually making it hard to perform well when you need to mingle. We also tend to spend time monitoring how we perform during social interactions, which also prevents us from paying proper attention to the conversation. Therefore, it is best to try to remove this tendency to focus on ourselves. There are a few ways to do this:

- Be yourself – there is no need to put up a front because you cannot please everyone at the same time.
- Don't worry too much about silences: Sure, we all dread awkward silences but everyone needs to keep the conversation going, not just you alone. Plus, silences do not need to be filled all the time.
- There is no need to perform perfectly during conversations, either. No one can achieve such a high standard.
- If you perform badly during any part of the interaction, do not reply to them in your head. Instead, just focus on what is being said in the present moment.
- While you are at it, try your best to concentrate on the conversation you are in. There is no room to think about how you

would look to others or how well you are performing.
- Also, you are not the central focus of everyone's attention. Others have plenty of things to think and talk about.
- While you might feel anxious during a conversation does not mean that you are doing badly.
- Even if you are visible anxious, others will not think badly of you. We all have experienced anxiety in our life and it does not alienate you.
- Anxiety is actually much less visible than you think.
- Try to spend less time focusing on your own physical symptoms in social situations.

From here, we can start to gradually confront the situations we often avoid. We can then move on to stopping avoidance and safety behaviors.

Stopping Avoidance and Safety Behaviors

When we feel anxious, we avoid social situations such as parties, asking for a refund, speaking in front of small groups, etc. However, as you should already know, the most you keep avoid the situations you fear, the lesser the chance you get to prove yourself that you can cope with them. Therefore, your confidence will remain low. Safety behaviors are also the same because they try to be as agreeable as possible. It helps in the short term, but they are actually damaging because socially anxious individuals will never know that they could have coped without relying on such behaviors. Therefore, safety behaviors are just as damaging as avoidance.

As such, the best way to reduce anxiety is to reduce it by gradually confronting them, without relying on avoidance or safety behaviors. You can call this exposure therapy, and you don't need a professional to do this. Of course, it is always daunting to confront social situations especially since we feel anxious when we do so. However, research shows that if we continue to expose ourselves to anxious-inducing situations long enough without using safety behaviors or avoidance, our anxiety will gradually reduce. It is as if our mind and body become used to the situation. This can take more than half an hour, but it can happen very quickly. Most importantly, when we are confronted with a similar situation again, we will not feel as anxious anymore. Moreover, our anxiety will be reduced faster and faster each time as well, until we no longer feel anxious.

For example, suppose that you feel anxious about spending time in the park because you feared that everyone would stare at you. How do you overcome this problem? The answer is simple. Take yourself to the park and hang out there until you no longer feel anxious. Then, repeat it every day that week. You will eventually feel less and less anxious and more and more confident.

Of course, anxiety will only remain for a short period of time when you have a brief chat with your neighbor in the street. While they are just as anxious-inducing because they happen spontaneously so you cannot prepare in advance, you can also get used to these brief moments if you allow yourself to get involved in these short moments instead of avoiding them. That way, you can prove to yourself that you can handle such scenarios better than you initially anticipated, thus increasing your confidence. Again, confronting social situations can be daunting. Thankfully, there are five steps you can take to make this easier.

Generating Ideas for Your Exposure Hierarchy

Because confronting social situations can be daunting, it is helpful to do it in a gradual way by creating an exposure hierarchy. An exposure hierarchy is a list of social situations which would make you feel anxious, starting with the least anxious to the most anxious situation as your confidence grow. If you do not know where to start, think of the scenarios that you avoid or escape from, or you only confront if you are using a safety behavior, or those that make you feel anxious.

It is critical that the scenarios in your list cause a different level of anxiety and that you start by confronting the easiest or least anxious-inducing item in your list. That way, you can work your way up easier.

Ranking your Hierarchy

When you have a list of items, the next step is to try and rank them in order of least anxious to most anxious-inducing scenarios. You can use the scale from 0 to 100 to predict how anxious how you would feel in those situations. 0 is the most relaxed you have ever felt, and 100 is the most anxious you have ever felt. Then, arrange them from the lowest to the highest score.

Confronting the First Item

When you have finished making your list, it is finally time to confront the first item as soon as possible. This should be relatively easy as it is the least anxiety provoking of them all. When you are confronting the items in your list, is important to remember that:

- Although your anxiety will rise during the exposure task, it will subside if you remain in that situation long enough
- Know that anxiety is a natural and healthy reaction that everyone experiences. It will be unpleasant, but it is not dangerous and will pass eventually
- Further down the line, you might find it hard to remain in an anxiety-provoking situation for a long time. If so, try to remain in that situation until your anxiety reduces by at least 50%. For example, if your anxiety rises to about 80 during the exposure task, try to remain there until it gets to 40. As always, this can take more than 30 minutes, but it can also subside quickly in most cases. It is also worth pointing out that, depending on the nature of

the social situation, it can be impossible to remain in it for a long time such as when you say hello to a stranger or talk to a neighbor on the way to your car. This is fine even though your anxiety will not rise and fall naturally. Repeated exposure to such situations will eventually make confronting them less anxiety provoking, which should make you more comfortable in similar situations in the future.

- Again, anxiety is not as noticeable as you think
- Avoid using safety behaviors as they slow your progress. If it is difficult to remove them all at once, try to reduce them over time
- Focus on the conversation and the people around you. Do not focus on your own performance or what others might be thinking

- It is also helpful to try to challenge any unhelpful thoughts first before you start the exposure task
- If you attempt an exposure task and it does not go well for you, do not think too much of it as this can happen from time to time. What you need is repeated exposure to the scenario, and you will eventually be comfortable with it.

It is also worth mentioning that not all social situations you get involved in will go the way you think. There is no way to predict them beforehand, so it can be impossible to follow your hierarchy exactly. For example, a stranger might approach you and ask for directions when you are not comfortable talking with strangers yet. This is absolutely fine, however. If you find yourself in such a situation, try your best to follow the pointers above. Also, it can be tricky to confront certain situations because they happen spontaneously and cannot be arranged or set up. This can be speaking to a group of people or asking a shop assistant for a refund. Here, you might need to be opportunistic and look out for opportunities to engage in such situations. Because they can be hard to come by, you should consider engaging in those situations even if they are far up the hierarchy.

Rinse and Repeat

When you have completed an exposure task, you need to do it again and again, as often as possible until you no longer feel anxious. As stated previously, you will find that it gets easier every time you expose yourself to the scenario. As a rule of thumb, try to do it every day. The more often you do so, the quicker you will overcome your fear towards it.

Move On

After completing the first item on your list, you should follow the same step for all of the items on the list. Continue through your hierarchy in this manner until you have completed all items on the list. By then, you should feel more confident about social situations.

When you progress through the list, your confidence will grow, so the things that initially seemed very frightening to you might not be as scary when you completed the previous exposure task.

If the exposure task is still too hard for you, maybe you missed something between the previous item and this one. See if you can find something in-between by building a step or two before it. This can help boost your confidence just enough so you can confront the item. For example, suppose that you have three items on your list: making eye contact with a stranger, and asking a stranger for directions, and ordering a pizza. If you find the second task to be too difficult, maybe you should break everything down. So, instead, there will be five activities: making eye contact with a stranger, saying hello to a stranger in the street, asking a stranger for directions, ordering a pizza over the phone, and ordering a pizza in person.

Also, if you find that your anxiety still has not been reduced since the initial exposure, ask yourself whether you are using a safety behavior. Again, safety behaviors can prevent you from confronting your fear.

Overcoming Shyness

All of us feel shy at one point or another. For some people, it can be so debilitating that it prevents them from participating in social situations, especially those that are critical to personal or professional goals. The reality is those shy people do not despise being with other people. They are just afraid of being rejected or criticized, which is often associated with being with other people. This sad reality caused them to avoid social events that they want to attend. As a result, they end up feeling lonely and isolated, which heightens their chance of developing other mental disorders such as depression or anxiety. Sometimes, those people try to overcome shyness with alcohol in a form of self-medicating, which helps in the short term, but actually increases their risk for substance use disorder when they become too dependent on alcohol.

Research shows that shyness is maintained through a vicious cycle in which individuals approach a social situation and feel the excessive fear of negative evaluation, and then avoid the situation entirely. This initially provides relief, but often leads to feelings of shame and self-blame. To cope with such reactions, our negative emotions may turn into anger and blame toward others, so they can be perceived as inconsiderate or unsupportive. Of course, this only further reinforces our desire to avoid them. Because social skills, just like any other sets of skills, are something we can develop over time, the avoidance of social settings can render us antisocial and make it hard for us to socialize the more we neglect them. Thankfully, there are four ways to improve your social skills:

Plan for It

Unlike introversion which is associated with being reserved and quiet, shyness is characterized by a strong tendency to overestimate negative scrutiny. We all fear that others will negatively evaluate us, so we tend to spend quite a lot of time thinking of what we did wrong instead of trying to do something right.

One quick way to reduce anxiety is by thinking about what you could do to improve the situation. If you are worried about making small talks, ask yourself a few questions to generate ideas. Think about some current events that you could bring up or mention something interesting in your life you feel comfortable sharing, or discuss the things that you have in common with other people there.

You should also have a viable exit strategy, but try your best not to use it. Exposing yourself to fear is the best way to overcome it, but you also need to feel in control of the situation. If you know that you have an exit strategy for the worst-case scenario, you will not feel trapped. The exit strategy is only there to make you feel safe. It is not meant to be used.

Be Curious

According to Dale Carnegie's "How to Win Friends and Influence People", the best first principle is to be genuinely interested in others. This principle is based on the work of psychologist Alfred Adler who wrote, "It is the individual who is not interested in his fellow men how has the greatest difficulties in life."

So, when you find yourself in a social setting, try to take your focus off yourself and instead focus on being curious about other people. Learn who they are and why there are there. Find out about their interests and hobbies. Not only that this gives you something different to focus on so you can generate conversation topics, but you might also learn a thing or two from them as well. Everyone has a story to tell and most of them are more than willing to share it with you if you just ask. Just sit back and listen. The only way to be the most interesting person in the room is to be interested in others.

Give Yourself a Role

Many socially shy individuals are actually very successful professionals, including lawyers, professors, business owners, and doctors. They are very confident at work, but they at not where their role is not defined by their jobs. A role gives you a sense of purpose and an idea for how you should behave. Anyone in any setting wants to feel liked and accepted. So, give yourself the role of making others feel the way they would like to feel. Your job is to help people feel interesting, liked, and welcomed.

How to Stop Beating Yourself Up

If you are like most people, you already know your inner critic too well. This is the voice that doubts you, belittles you, judges you, and tells you that you are not good enough all the time. It whispers things to you that other people would never say to you. Whether you like it or not, everything you say to yourself. While the voice will not physically harm you, it can ruin your life if you cannot keep it under control. Given enough time, it can lead to serious mental health problems such as depression or anxiety.

Of course, the inner critic can serve many purposes that might seem useful on the surface. The harsh messages it hurls at you is intended to make you push yourself to achieve more. However, this is like choosing a punishment over a reward if you use self-criticism for these reasons instead of positive self-talk. While you might argue that punishment can stop certain behaviors in the short-term, rewards are actually a lot more effective to shape new and lasting behaviors. When you punish someone for something they did wrong, that does not teach them how to do it right. When you blame someone for doing something poorly, it does not make them instantly better at it. Imagine a small child learning to walk, and whenever he falls down, his parents would yell and call him nasty names. That is a horrible sight, is it not? You can probably imagine what that would do to the child when he grows up. On the flip side, if the parents smile and encourage the child for each step he takes toward them, you can bet that it would have a very different effect. The same also applies to your inner critic. If it consistently labels you negatively, it will demoralize you and influence your self-image of who you are and what you can do.

Shy people are usually critical of themselves, and their inner voices are often very harsh on them. They would say things to themselves that they would never say to other people. When you judge yourself too harshly, you will likely assume that others will judge you just as harshly. Your inner critic can cause you a lot of emotional pain, robbing you of self-esteem and peace of mind.

Now, you might be wondering if the inner critic is telling the truth. The reality is that it does not matter if it is. Negative-self talk is never in your interest. There is always another way to treat yourself that does not involve negativity and self-destructive mindsets.

So, the best way to silence your inner critic is to have a more powerful voice on your side. This is an inner voice that acts like your best friend. You can do so by starting to notice good things about yourself and talk back to your inner critic. When it starts to blame you for being too fearful, remember that no one wants to be rejected, but we always survive it. When your inner critic tells you that no one will like you, remind yourself that what really matters is that you love yourself. When you learn to talk to yourself in a gentler, kinder way, social situations will not have as much power over you because you will not be punishing yourself. Let's break that down, shall we?

Notice the Critic

In order to take control of your inner critic, you need to be aware of its presence first. This is not hard because you have an inner dialogue with yourself during ever conscious moments. Most of our thinking is automatic and rapid that we might not notice it before we proceed to the next thought. So, you can notice the inner critic by slowing down and make a conscious effort to pay more attention to your own thoughts. Your emotions also give you clues to the presence of the critic. Whenever you feel doubtful, guilty, shameful, or worthless, then your inner critic is already at work.

So, for the first week, you can keep an inner critic log in a small notebook or your phone. When you notice that you are being critical of yourself, just write a few words about the situation such as "got up late", "fight with mom", "lunch choices", or "meeting with the boss", and what the criticism was about the situation. Maybe it is "I'm lazy, I'm a bad employee, I'm not a good son, I have no self-control," When you are aware of the inner critic, you can stand up to it.

Dissociate the Critic

Remember that your inner critic thrives best when you thought that it is a part of yourself. It does not want you to notice that it is there because you were not born with an inner critic. It is a voice that you internalized based on learning and external influence, such as other people's standards, expectations, and criticism. So, you can dissociate yourself from the critic by giving it a name. Any name will do, but you can use a silly name to add some levity like calling it The Mad Lad or The Old Hag. What matters is that when you separate it from your own identity by giving it a name, you are on your way to liberate yourself from its debilitating influence.

Talk Back

From there, you can start talking back to your inner critic to take away its power. You can just tell the critic that you do not want to hear whatever it has to say, which gives you a sense of choice in the matter. Whenever you hear the inner critic starting to talk, tell it to go away. Say that you refuse to listen and that you know it is a liar. Tell it that you choose to be kind to yourself instead.

Replace the Critic

Finally, you can defeat the inner critic by having a stronger ally on your side. You need to develop an inner voice that acts like your best friend. To achieve this, you need to start noticing the good things about yourself. While the inner critic has a lot of nasty things to say about you, you have plenty of positive things as well, though it can take some effort to see them. This is because of how our brains work. You see, we all have an automatic selective filtering system that will find evidence in our environment to prove whatever we believe to be true about ourselves. Then, we will disregard other evidence to the contrary. If you always tell yourself "I'm an idiot", you will zero in on the small mistakes that you make such as accidentally locking your keys inside your cars, even though you do a lot of other smart things. You tend to focus on the negative things because you say negative words to yourself.

So, to break this vicious cycle, you need to make a deliberate effort to say something different to yourself and actively look for evidence that supports the new positive statement about yourself. When your inner critic starts to say anything negative, tell it that it is not true. Then, replace that statement with something you know is true. For example, if your inner critic says that you are an idiot, say that you do a lot of smart things as well. Then, think of many examples to support that positive statement. Your inner critic does not like to be wrong, so the more examples you can think of to contradict the critic's negative statements, the less it will come around. Eventually, it will disappear.

How to Stop Anxiety Attacks

Experiencing anxiety attacks might be unnerving, and if we don't understand why or how our body produces an anxiety attack, we could only respond to it with more anxiety. This, which we already discussed, only lead to more anxiety attacks. So, how do we stop anxiety attacks?

Understand Anxiety Attacks

If you have read the first chapter, then you should have a pretty clear idea of what cause anxiety attacks. When you know exactly what anxiety attacks are, their causes, how your body responds to them, and how they affect your body, it no longer becomes the unknown. In some cases, you become frightened of anxiety attacks because you do not know exactly what is happening. You might be afraid of anxiety attacks exactly, but you are fearful of the unknown, and when you have familiarized yourself with anxiety attacks, their effects are drastically nullified.

Stop Scaring Yourself

As mentioned previously, anxiety attacks are mainly caused when you are afraid. Therefore, being afraid of them will not help you overcome anxiety attacks at all. Because fear is the main reason why anxiety attacks occur and persist, holding your ground and refuse to be scared of them remove the main reason why anxiety attacks occur. When you take the fear out of the picture, you will not fall victim to anxiety attacks as often.

For instance, when you are having anxiety attacks, use more affirmative language like "Okay, this doesn't feel right, but it's just my body being alarmed. It'll end eventually if I remain calm" instead of "Oh, God. This is awful. What if I completely lose it?"

Instead of thinking, "What is causing this terrible feeling? What if I'm dying or having a complete breakdown?" change that to, "This is a strong emotion I'm feeling, but it is harmless. It's only natural, but there's really nothing to worry about. It will pass eventually and I'll be fine!"

Or, instead of thinking, "This is awful. I can't stand this!" Instead think, "So this is what it feels like to be overly stressed. Everyone feels this sometimes. It's not dangerous."

When you take charge of your own thinking that way, you will eventually get better at shutting down anxiety attacks and prevent them from occurring.

Calm Yourself

Similar to the previous point, calming yourself helps shut down the mechanism that triggers anxiety attacks. Calming yourself down disrupts stress response, and then all you need to do let your body use the remaining stress hormones before it returns to normal.

The more you calm yourself down, the faster anxiety attacks will end and the sooner you will feel better. Remember that physiological, psychological, and emotional changes caused by a minor stress response can last for about ten minutes, while a high level of stress response can last for twenty minutes or longer. You need to keep calm during the anxiety attack until the body recovers. That means that you will still experience physiological, psychological, and emotional changes during the anxiety attack, but they will eventually pass as the body recovers from the stress response. Therefore, calming yourself down is another great way to shut down, and prevent anxiety attacks.

During moments when things seem out of control or moving too fast, take three deep breaths. In fact, the first thing everyone should do when they are emotional or losing control is by taking a few deep breaths. It allows them to calm the mind down and allow the emotion to blow over, therefore letting them make calm and collected decisions.

If possible, it is recommended to practice Diaphragmatic breathing. As the name suggests, it is a relaxation technique by breathing from the diaphragm rather than the chest. Basically, the stomach should rise up instead of the chest and shoulder when practicing this technique.

It is a common practice for athletes to breathe from their mouth when they are running. Doing so forces them to breathe unconsciously from their stomach. Almost everyone is used to breathe from the chest. These breaths are often short and quick and only deliver a small amount of air to the lungs, resulting in gaining a minimal amount of oxygen to the bloodstream. Chest breathing often kicks in during hyperventilation or when the person feels out of breath because it helps to take in as much oxygen as possible very quickly. Public speakers are often told to breathe from their stomach because it helps them talk longer and maintain a smooth, deep voice. Everyone should have a habit of breathing from their stomach since it also serves as a passive stress relief method. Stomach breathing uses the entire lung capacity, maximizing the oxygen intake at the cost of slower breathing. At the same time, carbon dioxide is also pushed out of the body at the fastest rate.

Diaphragmatic breathing is a good way to relax and reduce anxiety of various kinds. It is best to consult with a doctor before beginning this relaxation training exercise for those with medical conditions.

First, find a quiet and peaceful place with no distractions. Then, lay down on the floor or recline in a chair. If wearing any tight clothing, loosen it and remove glasses or contacts. Put the hands on the lap or on the armrest. Then, put a hand on the upper chest and another on the stomach. Inhale slowly to draw in a deep breath. When inhaling, the stomach should rise up and the chest should not move. Hold the breath for a bit before exhaling while counting to three. The stomach should slowly fall back down. Then, continue this pattern for about 10 minutes.

Some people find it hard to maintain deep breaths for 10 minutes and their breaths often become shallow again. It is possible that the current practice is not a perfect moment for practicing diaphragmatic breathing. If that is the case, try taking a yoga class or sing up for a mindfulness meditation course. There are also voice recordings out there to help those who struggle with this relaxation technique. Their purpose is to help people fully relax and concentrate on the technique.

A good way to incorporate this breathing exercise into a daily routine is by setting up a reminder on the phone at a convenient time. The idea is to have a habit of breathing from the diaphragm instead of the chest. Relaxing your body also shuts off the stress response because it is impossible to be relaxed and excited at the same time. The more relaxed you are, the faster your body uses up the stress hormones that will bring an end to the associated emotions with an active stress response. Relaxing your body also reduces the muscle tension caused by the stress response.

Distract Yourself

As mentioned earlier, most of your anxiety attacks are caused and fueled by your anxious thoughts. You can counter this by distracting yourself, focusing your attention on something else so your anxious thoughts That way, you can stop voluntary anxiety attacks.

Thankfully, there are plenty of ways to distract yourself, such as counting to ten, calling a friend, tidying up your home, organizing your working desk, playing a video game, reading a book, etc. Anything that you can think of to distract the anxious thoughts will help.

Sometimes, you need to engage your senses to distract yourself. Maybe you need a cold or warm shower. Maybe you need to eat some ice-cream or your favorite food. Maybe you need to snuggle up in a blanket. These sensory experience helps to distract yourself and these can reduce the sensations associated with the active stress response.

Other Things to Remember

During panic attacks, it can be easy to lose control over yourself. When that happens, no matter how strong the anxiety attack is, remember that it will eventually end. It is a reassuring thought when you know that whatever terrible emotions you are experiencing, they will eventually end. As mentioned earlier, it can take some time before your anxiety attack subsides. No one experiences a perpetual anxiety attack even though it might feel that way. Riding out your anxiety attack knowing that it will end can help you stay calm.

Stress and survival mechanism in itself is not really a bad thing. Many people actually seek the rush of the stress response. That is why skydiving, bungee jumping, or other dangerous but thrilling activities exist. Therefore, a high degree of stress response is not really a bad thing. In reality, it is our body's response to a dangerous situation to survive. We can shut this response down anytime by practicing the above strategies.

While you are panicking, remember that you are in control of your own emotions. The above strategies will help you maintain control. It will take some effort and courage to start practicing these techniques initially, but you can control your anxiety and anxiety attacks.

Activities to Get Better

Social anxiety activities are intended to challenge your anxiety in various ways. Social anxiety disorder affects up to 13% of the world's population, and socially anxious individuals suffer in all areas of their lives. They face difficulties making or maintaining friends, finding life partners, finding work and building their careers. In certain cases, they may even have problems going through the mundane aspects of their daily lives.

While social anxiety disorder can be destructive, and some of the best treatments involve the combination of cognitive-behavioral therapy and medication, there are other things you can do to help yourself overcome social anxiety.

Self-help strategies often draw on the effective components of other, more traditional treatment approaches. They may utilize aspects of relaxation, thought reprogramming, and exposure to situations as we have already discussed.

If you find yourself a victim of mild to moderate social anxiety, and most socially anxious individuals are, you might just feel like you are in the ditch most of the time. What is the best way to get yourself out of the ditch? Well, you do something about it.

Put Yourself Out There

We already talked about exposure therapy and avoidance previously, and how they do not help the situation at all. We want to stress again that practice makes perfect. In fact, Dr. Jordan B. Peterson once said in his YouTube video when asked about what a socially anxious individual should do, and his first response is, "Put yourself out there, man." Let's be honest here. No matter how many times you read these self-help books or watch videos on how to overcome social anxiety and improve social skills, you can never improve without practicing. That is why exposure therapy works so well. That means accepting invitations and going places that make you uncomfortable. Sure, you may feel horrible at the end of the day, but you should see the edge of your comfort zone as a place you can improve. It is not a dead end. It is an area of improvement. At the same time, you also need to prepare yourself to properly handle being out there.

Improve Your Health

Your health is critical to improving your social skills and overcoming social anxiety. You need to do everything in your power to ensure that poor physical health is not a contributing factor to your social anxiety. Exercise regularly, eat a healthy, balanced diet, etc. Stay away from caffeine and alcohol. You can also drink chamomile tea to calm your nerves.

If you are not already exercising regularly, consider planning a program for yourself today. Exercise increases your feelings of well-being, not to mention reducing anxiety. If you hit the gym, you will also have the added benefit of socializing with strangers in a low-risk environment. If you do not have the resources nor time to join a gym or regular exercise classes, there are still plenty of things you can do alone or right at home. You can go for a walk or run around the block, which helps freshen your mind. If not, you can even exercise right at home, and there are plenty of YouTube videos out there. You can also practice yoga or meditation at home, which we have already discussed.

Keep a Journal

Have a daily journal handy so you can write down your feelings and see how much you have improved over time. Writing about your thoughts and experiences also help you recognize when you are going back to the old, destructive ways.

While you are at it, make sure to write down your goals about what you want to achieve. You should not have vague goals. They should be SMART, as in specific, measurable, attainable, realistic, and time-specific. It can be overcoming symptoms of social anxiety or become an award-winning actress. Whatever it is, it is important to put your goals down on paper, making them real and measurable.

A part of goal setting involves thinking of where you want to end up, but it also involves learning and setting a benchmark of where you currently are. One way to do that is by taking some self-assessment quizzes to see how well you score in terms of social anxiety. You should give the Liebowitz scale a shot. From there, you can work on yourself and take the quiz again in a month or so to see how well you have improved. Remember that you should not compare yourself to others in terms of social success. This is because other people lead a different life and comparing yours to theirs is pointless. Plus, you do not know what the other person is going through. You would never know them enough, so you should not measure yourself to them. You should, instead, measure yourself to someone you know well. Who is that? You, of course. Compare yourself to who you were yesterday, last week, last month, or last year.

If you see that you have improved, then congratulate yourself. There are actually a lot of things about you that you should be proud of.

Remember that you face unique challenges and overcoming them is no small feat. You should feel good about yourself for even the smallest accomplishments in your life, especially if you have social anxiety.

Be Your Own Best Advocate

No one is going to take care of you the way you can take care of yourself. Treat yourself as if you are someone who you care about or who you are responsible for taking care of. Would you ensure that your dog visits the vet regularly and gets enough exercise, healthy food, and medication? Only a few wouldn't. So why would you not visit the doctor or dentist regularly? Why would you not get enough exercise and eat enough healthy food? So, gather knowledge about social anxiety disorder so you can make better decisions. Make your needs known. Be assertive (more on that later). Ask for accommodations at work and school if you think that they will help you out. Explain your struggles to others so they would understand.

Take time out at parties when you need to. After all, no one knows you better than yourself.

Ask for help if you must, from a friend or a professional. Do not wait until tomorrow or next week, or until you are in desperate need for help. Make an appointment to see someone. If you are too embarrassed to see your doctor, why not calling a mental health helpline? There should be one in your country. They will help you get started. Talking to an anonymous stranger on the phone is actually less intimidating and it may be the help you need. Just take the first step and reach out. You should not keep everything bottled up, though. If possible, consider talking to your friends, family, or those you know love and care about you.

Herbal Supplements

Herbal supplements are used occasionally to help relieve anxiety. You may have been told to use a few of these, and some are commonly used in the treatment of social anxiety disorder. While these herbal supplements lack scientific evidence backing up their effectiveness, you may find that some of them may actually help with certain symptoms.

Remember, if you are considering taking herbal supplements to treat your social anxiety, remember that there is little to no scientific evidence currently supporting the effectiveness of these alternative medicines. Other than that, the U.S. Food and Drug Administration does not regulate its production, and they are not thoroughly tested, meaning that there is no guarantee regarding the ingredients or safety of the products.

Basically, before you take any herbal remedies, consult with a qualified healthcare provider about potential interactions before you commit and regret it a day later. You should also look for Supplements Facts label on the product that you buy, which will tell you vital information regarding the number of active ingredients per serving, and other added ingredients. You should also look and only purchase supplements with a seal of approval from a reputable third-party organization such as the U.S. Pharmacopeia,

ConsumerLab.com, and NSF International. While the label does not mean that the product is 100% safe, it at least assures you that the product was properly manufactured, contains the ingredients as listed, and does not contain harmful levels of contaminants.

Chamomile

Chamomile tea should be common if you live in North America. You should drink some before bed to get its calming and sedating effects, although these are not proven by any scientific studies. However, the placebo effect is a thing and you should have a cup of something warm before bed anyway, so chamomile tea is not a bad idea, unless you have allergies, have bleeding disorders or take drugs that may increase the risk of bleeding, or are pregnant and nursing women because chamomile may act as a uterine stimulant, and may lead to the fetus being aborted.

Kava Kava

Unlike Chamomile, there is actually some clinical evidence that associate kava kava with anxiety reduction. However, because it has the potential to damage the liver, many countries have issued safety warnings or outright banned this supplement. If you want to use kava kava, consult with your doctor and the law first. Kava kava is not recommended at all if you have liver disease, liver problems, or are currently taking medications that affect the liver.

Passion Flower

Passion flower is a climbing vine native to southeastern North America, and its flowers, leaves, and stems are used to create the herbal supplement. There are only a few animals and human studies on this supplement, but they suggest that passion flower may be effective if used to treat anxiety, insomnia, and nervous disorder. Just like Chamomile, more scientific studies are needed to confirm or disprove their effects. Just like any other herbal remedies, it is not a good idea to take passion flower if you are pregnant, breastfeeding, or taking other medications.

RhodiolaRosea

The plant, which is also known as golden root or arctic root, actually thrives in dry and cold climates such as Siberia. It has been classified by some researchers as an adaptogen, meaning that it can make you less prone to physical and emotional stress. It has been shown to stimulate serotonin, norepinephrine, and dopamine activity, which may treat depression, fatigue, and improve exercise performance. Again, more scientific studies are needed. While RhodiolaRosea is usually taken in capsule form, you can find it as extracts and teas.
St. John's Wort

With a name like that, it is no surprise to see why it is a popular herbal supplement. It is used primarily to treat mild to moderate depression. It is to be taken in pills form. Again, there is no clinical or scientific evidence backing up its effectiveness, with one back in 2005 suggests that it is not any more effective than placebo. As always, consult with your doctor or a qualified healthcare provider before you take this one.

Valerian Root

Valerian root has been used for thousands of years as a remedy for digestive problems, sleep problems, nervous disorders, and many other ailments. Nowadays, it is used mainly as a sleep aid. It comes in capsule, tea, tablet, or liquid extract and it should be taken 30 minutes to two hours before bedtime. It still lacks the scientific evidence backing its effectiveness, so you should practice caution similar to those recommended above.

Confront Your Fear

A quick google search will tell you that there are many methods you can employ to cope with and manage your social anxiety. We have covered them extensively in this book, and this technique we are about to talk about here has also been proven to be effective. It involves making yourself vulnerable, but instead of turning the other way, you face it head-on. That way, fear,and anxiety are drained of their debilitating power. Here are the things you need to do.

So What?

First, you need to rewire your thinking from "what-ifs" to "whatever". For example, "What if they hate me?" to "If they do, then whatever. If they hate me, then I probably should not be their friends. They have nothing personal against me. It's just that they will not get along with me. I can't please everyone anyway." When you think this way, it helps you stop overthinking when anxiety starts creeping in.

This is basically accepting the reality of the situation instead of the speculations you make in your head. "It is what it is," is the name of the game here. You need to calm yourself and not be unnerved by whatever will happen next.

Accept It

We mentioned earlier that you should not bottle up your feelings. Just like meditation, you should be with your feelings. Be aware of how you are feeling and let the sensation of anxiety runs through you for a while. Do not try to fight it. Accept the feelings and allow your body to accept the anxious feelings from a fast heartbeat to that dizziness. It will be uncomfortable but just go through it.

Face It

From there, welcome the anxiety with opens and be happy about it. Okay, this sounds a bit weird because why would anyone be happy about having anxiety? After all, there is nothing really fun about anxiety. However, when you do that, you actually externalize anxiety, meaning that you manage to dissociate yourself from anxiety. Plus, there is yet another added benefit of doing this. When you run towards it, eventually you will no longer be afraid of it. Having a strong mentality like "Bring it on, sucker! Is that all you got?" when you face your anxiety automatically shuts down panic attacks. Your mind physically cannot create anxiety on your demand.

From the outside, though, you would look like you are sitting normally while you run over your anxiety. This is the battle that you should fight inside your head. Allow yourself to feel it, and then scoff at how harmless it really is.

Do Other Activities

Finally, take your time to physically engage in other activities. The more engaged your mind is, the less anxious you will feel and the less powerful anxiety becomes. Basically, after you have proven to yourself and your anxiety that it is harmless, you can ignore it and goes on to do other things.

Chapter 4: Mindfulness and Relaxation Techniques

Whether we like it or not, we all worry about so much. There are big things like relationships or career or your direction in life, or it can be mundane, insignificant things such as your to-do list. While worrying is completely normal, but if you worry all the time, it will stop you from really experiencing and enjoying what is happening at the moment, and it can develop into anxiety and panic attack.

Because life is fast-paced, you will find that you spend most of your time in your head, thinking. We plan, analyze, and set goals at work. We compare, label, and judge our experience. We spend a lot of time dwelling in the past and anticipate what could happen in the future. Our mind is constantly telling stories, interpreting our experience by filling in the gaps and ruminating over the stories it has crafted, regardless of its validity.

When you are lost in your own worries, it is very easy to see them as facts instead of recognizing them as mere thoughts. This is compounded when your thoughts become so real that you have an emotional or even physical response to them. You might think that your boss or your friend not calling you back means that they hate you or something when the reality is that they are just having a busy day. You might get caught up imagining the worst when you go for an interview or giving a presentation. Such anxious provoking thoughts may lead to shallow breaths, butterflies in the stomach, or lightheadedness. Before you realize what is really going on inside your head, you are already panicking as a reaction to your thoughts. This can interfere with your sleep, your body's ability to digest and repair, and make you feel exhausted.

If you worry about so many things, then you are not alone. Thankfully, you can do something about it. When you shift your attention from your thoughts and into your body experience and the sensations of breathing, you can get your head out of the clutter and into a sensing mode. This alters your physical, emotional, and psychological response. This is known as meditation, and it is intended to slow down your thoughts and clear your head. We mentioned previously that you should not focus on your own sensations during conversations. You should, however, do so when you worry too much when you are alone.

If you, just like many others, become upset, frustrated, or angry with yourself for worrying, anxious, or panicky, and resist what you are experiencing, you will know that this only intensifies the anxiety, making it a lot worse. Rather than denying the experience by telling yourself that you should not be feeling whatever you are feeling right now or trying not to feel or get upset, remember that you need to allow yourself to feel your raw emotions. If you acknowledge what you are feeling and allow it to manifest momentarily, it is easier for you to settle down and let it pass. The best way to achieve that is through meditation. This mindfulness practice helps you retake control of your mind and steer it into a more positive frame of mind.

Mindfulness has been a subject of study in clinical, professional sports, military, and corporate settings for over 30 years now. The research found that mindfulness is associated with a significant number of benefits such as increased job performance and reduction in stress and anxiety. Many scholars agree that mindfulness is a state of consciousness consisting of awareness and attention. Mindfulness is comprised of three things:

- A clear focus of attention on the present moment, including experience and events
- Ability to change the level of non-judgmental attention
- Awareness of changing attention between the inner self and the outer world

Basically, mindfulness is achieved by focusing your attention on your actions, feelings, and thoughts as they occur. To strengthen your emotional self-awareness, you need to start practicing mindfulness training, which is characterized by the ability to recognize your own emotions and how they influence our feelings. While there are plenty of mindfulness practices out there, some really good ones can last for eight weeks, we want to focus on something quick and convenient so you can do it right at home.

Meditation

The entire process is actually very simple and personalized. You might already be told to take deep breaths to keep your emotions under control. Meditation is basically deep breathing, but with a few extra steps with greater benefits as it allows you to take a look deep inside yourself and understand yourself better. It should not take too much time to prepare everything. However, if you want to reap the lasting benefits of meditation, you need to dedicate or find a permanent place where you will meditate.

The Props

Meditation will be a lot easier if you have a few items. There are plenty out there that claim to help you meditate, but there is no need to go overboard. All you need is a seat, a timer, and a place to meditate.

For your seating options, there are three options. You can sit on a chair or sofa if you are starting out with meditation, have back problems, or find meditation cushion uncomfortable. A chair or sofa keeps your back straight in sitting position as it is crucial in any meditation, though it is easier to snooze off and it can be tempting to just lean back instead of keeping your back straight, therefore making you lose focus. As such, consider switching to a meditation cushion when you are more familiar and comfortable with meditation.

A meditation cushion is the most common thing that people sit on when they meditate. It is so popular because of the fact that it is the easiest to sit on with an upright position. That, in turns, helps you stay alert and keep the quality of the meditation high. Of course, a meditation cushion does not have a backrest, but when you slump against it, you will lose focus. The meditation cushion helps you keep your back straight, maintaining that healthy posture without compromising focus.

You should try out the meditation bench if you are tall, have legs problems or that meditation cushion is just too uncomfortable and counterproductive to your meditation. Just like the meditation cushion, you still need to sit upright without the backrest so you cannot lean back and lose your focus. What makes this different from the meditation cushion is that it absorbs more weight than the cushion, so it takes off the pressure from your legs, and make meditation more comfortable for you.

The timer is another crucial tool to help you meditate. When you close your eyes and go on a journey of self-discovery that is meditation, it is easy to lose track of time, or overestimate how long have you been meditating. Stopping now and again to check the time is counterproductive, so have a timer ready. Because it is built into most smartphones, there really is no need for you to buy a physical meditation timer. All that you really need from the timer is to tell you when you should stop meditating so you don't have to break away from the trance just to look at the time.

Location is also crucial for your meditation. You need to find a place with enough light (but not too much), and with enough space, for you to be able to open up and let the fresh air comes through. Moreover, the place should allow you to unwind and feel relaxed before you start meditation. Therefore, use a light color for the wall and decoration. Again, there is no need to go over the top. A monotonous color with simple decorations like a vase is enough. Too many decorations and too many pictures painted on the wall might distract you instead. One more thing to consider is the noise. It should be kept at a minimum level so you will not get distracted.

Meditating

If you have watched any clips about meditation, you know that there are several forms of meditation. Do not fret. It is true that not much is said about how exactly to meditate, and beginners often worry if they are even sitting correctly, it all boils down to personal preference, hence the fact that there is little instruction. However, they share some common postures.

Close the eyes fully or keep them partially open. If you can focus on your breathing with your eyes closed, do that. If you feel sleepy with your eyes closed, open your eyes a bit and focus on the nearest object in your sight. Experiment and see what works for you.

For your head, tilt it slightly upward so to open up your body and helps it relax. Plus, it takes pressure off your neck when you lean your head back a bit, not to mention that it helps with your bad neck posture (slumping forward).

For your hands and legs, put them wherever you feel the most comfortable. You can put them on your laps or knees, put one palm over the other, or intertwine your fingers. The same also applies to your legs. You can cross your legs, put them in a pretzel-like position, or just put them normally when you sit on a chair.

While there are several types of meditations, you should follow a form that is most comfortable for you that still allows you to remain alert. Comfort and alertness should be your top priority. If you are uncomfortable, it will be hard to concentrate. If you are too comfortable, you might lose focus and fall asleep. Find that perfect balance that allows you to be comfortable but alert at the same time. In the end, the pose, form, or placements of hands and legs are up to you. You choose which one is the best for you, and stick to it.

When you have found the perfect meditation place and get into a comfortable position, set the timer. If you are a beginner, you should only meditate for only five minutes (it is longer than you think), and then work your way up. Meditation might seem easy to you, but it is actually pretty tricky. That is why not many people get into meditating. When you feel comfortable with five minutes, bump the number up to ten or even thirty minutes.

Now, start breathing and let your body relax. Focus on breathing. Focus on any aspect of your breathing that works for you. It can be how the air enters and exits your nose, how the air inflates and deflates your lungs, or how your stomach heaves up and down. If you have scented up your meditation place, focus on that. Remember that pacing is important to keep your breathing slow and steady. Take slow, deep breaths, and keep your mind empty.

Keeping your mind empty is a lot easier said than done, however. We are all used to think so much that not thinking is alien for our brain. It is very easy to get distracted. However, do your very best to focus your attention on your breathing, but do not be stressed if you do not do very well. Continue to focus on your breathing, and should your mind wander, just guide it back to the meditation. If it is hard to remain focused when you exhale, it is possibly because it is a lot subtler than inhaling. If that is the case, you can count whenever you exhale. From one to five, then back to zero. If focusing on your breathing is hard, or what you want to spice things up, then there are other alternatives that you could try out. You could try to focus on a certain part of the body at a time. Be aware of how that body part feels. You can even try to work your way up from your feet up to your head during meditation. Alternatively, you can place your attention on the light in the room. You can even switch up your point of focus on a daily basis. One day, you focus on the sounds, and the next day, you can focus on the light.

Additional Tips

There are also a few more things you need to remember when you meditate.

First, try to include meditation into your morning routine and bedtime routine. That way, you will not forget to do it daily. Doing so creates a transition period in the morning where your body will go from a relaxed state to an active state, and back to a relaxed state in the evening before you go to sleep. While you can simply skip meditation and launch yourself into the day full of stressful events, your body might not catch on and you will feel tired, making it hard to focus on your work. At the end of the day, meditation allows your body to relax so you can get a more restful sleep.

If you are a beginner, starting out with guided meditation is a good idea. Basically, it helps beginners and experts alike unlock the key to inner peace. But, you should not rely on it every time when you meditate.It is helpful in itself, you should learn how to access that place of silence and peace on your own. Otherwise, your own journey is not worth it. Of course, that does not mean that you should avoid this one like the plague. You just need to maintain a healthy balance between the guided meditations and traditional meditations. There are four main types of guided meditation. Traditional one gives instructions to guide your meditation process. The guided imagery will encourage you to use your imaginative power to visualize objects, scenes, or journey. The relaxation one is just music or natural sounds you can listen to so to relax your entire body. Affirmation meditation is intended to feed yourself positive thoughts.

As you meditate, a lot of things will come up in your mind, both good and bad. Observe them as if they are there to help you and develop positive thinking by seeing everything in a kind, and loving way. While your mind is showing you everything, try to take note of what pops up as they can be the source of your anger, anxiety, or frustration. You will recognize them as they present themselves. It is true that you should brush them aside as you meditate, you should remain with your thoughts for a moment because they have a reason to show up. They can actually help you pinpoint your problems which you can address later. Moreover, remember that meditation is more than relaxation. It is a journey of self-discovery. So, when you meditate, be aware of your own thoughts because they can be responsible for your behavior. Observe, but never judge nor criticize yourself. See yourself in a friendly way and give yourself love and try to understand yourself.

If you are just a beginner in meditation, then do not worry if you get distracted now and again during your meditation. The reality is that there is no way you could meditate perfectly. There will always be flaws. Your mind will wander sometimes, and that is completely fine. When that happens, just guide it back to your breathing. You will get better at it eventually. The only issues many beginners face is that they do not commit to meditation. They tried it once or twice, but then give up and say that meditation does not help them at all. In fact, it does, but it just takes time and effort. Try your best to develop a habit of meditation on a daily basis, and you will soon notice the difference.

After you have meditated, don't forget to smile. Meditation is also a process of giving yourself the attention you need and deserve. Smiling develops positive thinking as well. Be thankful for yourself that you allow yourself some quality time to meditate. Give yourself a pat on the shoulder. Everyone needs some self-love, and this is one of the ways to feed yourself that love.

Common Mistakes

There are many ways to meditate, that much is true. Certain of meditation can be modified to fit your own preferences, although some would try to add as many bells and whistles as possible. However, there are a few things you need to avoid when you meditate.

First and most importantly, never judge your own experience. When you meditate, the goal is to keep your breathing steady and your head clear. The purpose of meditation is to give your head and heart a break. It is also the practice of patience and gratitude at the same time. We already discussed the fact that you need to keep your mind and heart at peace when you meditate, and beginners often worry that they meditate wrong. Of course, we already talked about how worrying is not going to help you. So, instead of worrying, stop and focus on the fact that you are practicing meditation. Focus on yourself and the stillness of emotions. Let the silence soothe you.

A quick google search will show that there are many "meditation" necessities that you should buy in order to attain complete mindfulness. Now, you might be tempted to buy them so you could get the most out of your sessions, but they are just marketing scam at best. Remember that people used to meditate by sitting on the floor in an open room with enough air, and not much else. You will do just fine without those extra props. It is all about inner peace and external objects are irrelevant. Still, if some of them help, then you can keep some of them around. Just try to keep them to a minimum. Keep the ones that help you focus and relax.

Another problem with the modern world is the fact that we love to complicate things. Now, you can find hundreds of meditation techniques that have modern twists on ancient practices. While science has contributed to these modern variations, it is worth noting that they may lack the spiritual experience. Traditional meditation techniques have been developed and have thousands of years of experience in spiritual growth, and that makes them a better choice for serious practitioners. Modern meditation techniques can be fun to try out, but you should stick to the traditional ones. Still, we recommend you start with guided meditations first because it is a lot easier for you to develop a habit of meditating. These kinds of meditations help you unlock the key to inner peace easier, but you should move on to the traditional practice as soon as possible. While guided meditation helps for beginners, you need to learn how to access that place of silence and peace on your own. Otherwise, your journey is not worthwhile. Start with guided meditation and then transition slowly to traditional meditations.

After meditating for a while, you will start to feel that meditating is boring. Sometimes, you might start to feel that it is becoming a chore. By then, you might not want to meditate or even become more stressed about it. How do you avoid this problem? Simple. You can mix things up to keep it interesting. Consider meditating with your eyes open or with soothing ambient music once in a while if you haven't already. If you feel adventurous, try meditating when you are working. All you need to do is keep your head clear and take deep and steady breaths. You do not even need to sit down in a meditating position to start meditating. Just make sure that you are comfortable with the environment before you start.

Progressive Muscle Relaxation

Progressive muscle relaxation is a deep meditation that operates under the assumption that the muscles tense up in response to stressful thoughts. By relaxing the muscles, it is possible to release the built-up stress inside as well. It is also an effective way to relieve insomnia and reduce symptoms of certain types of chronic pain.

This relaxation technique works to counter the infamous fight-or-flight reaction that causes a lot of stress and anxiety. This response is a common reaction to fear or danger, which is hardly the case in reality. Nowadays, some harmless situations can trigger this response and it triggers physical symptoms such as accelerated heart rate, sweating, shaking, and shortness of breath thanks to the stress hormones. Since muscle pain, stiffness, and tension are common symptoms of stress and anxiety, this relaxation relieves stress by addressing those symptoms. It forces a relaxation response, calming the mind and lowering the heart rate by practicing slow, deep breathing and muscle relaxation routines.

This technique was described by Edmund Jacobson in about 1930. It is based upon his premise that mental calmness is a natural result of physical relaxation. Progressive muscle relaxation is very easy to learn and it only requires from 10 to 20 minutes a day to practice. While these techniques are effective against a wide number of conditions, some of which cannot be treated by medicine, it is worth noting that it can take a lot of therapy session to complete.

Progressive muscle relaxation is useful for treating conditions that medicine fails to cure, such as dementia. Even if the condition can be treated, some people prefer practicing these techniques than taking medicine because there is little or no risk associated with them. These techniques serve as a useful supplementary treatment for some psychological conditions as well. It is shown to be effective against withdrawal symptoms such as craving.

PMR: Step by Step

Start by finding a quiet place free from distractions. Lay down on the floor or recline in a chair. Loosen any tight clothing and remove glasses or contacts. Put the hands on the laps or on the arms rest. Then, take in a few deep breaths slowly. It is recommended to do a diaphragmatic breathing exercise throughout the entire exercise by synchronizing the breaths with the tension and the relaxation of the muscle in each area, but do not hold the breath. Some people find it more comfortable to work from the top of their head down to their toes. Others prefer doing it in the opposite direction. While this guide follows the former direction, it is still applicable to the latter method. Just like meditation, it is important to focus on each area of the muscle as it tightens and relaxes. It is okay if the mind wanders. Just guide it back to the muscle and proceed normally. Another thing worth noting is that one should not tighten the muscles to strain it.

Starting with the forehead muscle by raising the brows as high as possible, hold for about 5 seconds and then quickly release that tension. Give it a 5 to 10 seconds break and then move on to the cheek muscle. Smile as widely as possible. The mouth and cheeks should feel tense. Hold for 5 seconds and release quickly again. Do the same with the head by gently pulling it back to look at the ceiling, hold, release, and pause.

Moving down to the hand, clench the right fist, hold, release, and pause. Do the same to the right forearm, the upper arm, and then the entire arm. Make sure that the muscle in each area is tightened and feel the tension and relaxation. Do the same for the shoulders by lifting them as high up as possible. Repeat the process for the left hand, and then do the shoulders again.

Then, tense the upper back by pulling the shoulders back, hold, release, and pause. Work on the lower back by arching it. Then, do the same for the buttocks. After that, work on the legs by first tensing the entire right leg and thigh. Pull the toes inside and feel the tension in the calves. Repeat for the left leg.

Finally, bring the entire relaxation session to a close by feeling a wave of relaxation going from the head to toe. Relax and breathe slow and deep breaths for a few minutes.

Other Ways to Cultivate Mindfulness

There are more to mindfulness than meditation and progressive muscle relaxation techniques. You can incorporate the following techniques into your daily lives so you can get that peace of mind almost anywhere you go.

Change The Phone's Background

An average person spends about 4 years staring at their phone. Start by putting a "Breathe" on the background as a reminder. That way, the user is reminded to take a deep breath every time they look into their phone. While it may not seem much, taking a deep breath could alleviate some stress and allow the user to be present in the moment.

Set Reminder

Technology has caused humanity a considerable amount of stress in the workplace. Although it seems that technology has caused many distractions, it can be used in a productive way as well. It may seem counterintuitive because technology has made humans less mindful. However, by getting a bit creative, the power of technology can be harnessed to train the mind to be more mindful and aware. The best way to do it is similar to changing the phone's background. Try setting a gentle alarm or reminder to remind the mind to be present in the moment at least once every hour.

Change the Email Signature

Working with emails has become so boring that many people ignore most of the messages in it and change the part where it matters. The salutation and signature of emails have become almost meaningless. Although most of the email will be overlooked, try to use "With gratitude" as the email signature. It is true that the signature might be ignored, but it serves as a reminder as well.

Savor the Moment

One of the greatest tip to weight-loss is eating slowly. The same thing could be done here for a different purpose. Eating slowly is a perfect example of being grateful for what is already in one's possession. One could practice mindfulness by focusing on eating or drinking at least once a day. Instead of looking at the phone or TV, focus on the flavor of the food or drink. Savor every flavor. The same could be done when relaxing. Instead of zoning out and doing nothing, try to feel the moment when laying on the couch. During a vacation, take in the scenery and the fresh air instead of just taking photos and selfies.

Appreciate

The best way to practice mindfulness is by focusing on being aware of the smaller, insignificant things in life that might otherwise be overlooked. While they may be unimportant, they do add colors to people's lives. This is a very effective practice that should be utilized by billionaires, monks, and stoics because it assists them to appreciate the beauty of life and helps reduce anxiety. By simply thinking about one thing that would be missed for not having on a daily basis helps bring the mind to live in the present.

Another alternative to remaining in the moment that helps establish a bond with other people is by remembering that this time together could be the last one. It may seem a bit extreme or dark, but it is an effective way to encourage people to engage in meaningful conversation with each other. How much would that person be missed if they were to suddenly disappear one day? It is not implying that they will die one day, but the thought of not being able to talk to that person ever again after this makes people want to make their final moments together meaningful. This practice doubles as a helpful technique for those who have trouble sympathizing or socializing with other people.

Mindful Driving

Another thing that people tend to do mindlessly is that they hardly pay attention to their body when they are driving. Many people do not remember most of the details of their last drive. Such moments are perfect to practice mindfulness because a car serves as one filter from the noises of the outside world, not to mention that mindfulness allows the driver to focus on the road at all times – which is actually what they should be doing.

Next time, try to notice the steering wheel at the palm and feel the pressure under the foot as the car zips along the road. Use the lights as a reminder to remain in the present moment.

Mindfulness is a very simple and quick habit that many people can pick up. It is easy to personalize and any techniques are effective as long as they help bring the mind into living in the present. It may seem strange at first because the mind is so used to worrying and calculating future outcomes that it forgets to be present in the moment. By sparing less than 10 minutes every day to practice mindfulness techniques for about 21 days, a habit will be formed.

Mindfulness alone is enough to reduce stress. As stated earlier, though, in order to change one's life, one must have a meaning to do it. After all, while habits compel a person to continue doing something regularly, it is motivations that get them to take action. To many people, mindful practices for the benefits of reducing stress alone is not enough to motivate them. In such a case, mindful practices could be linked to spirituality. It is merely a question of value for people when it comes to belief, but since spirituality is an important element in many people's lives, one could use it as a reason to start their mindful routines.

Other Noteworthy Things about Mindfulness

Some people believe that mindfulness is elimination of thought because bringing people to the present moment must mean eliminating thoughts of the future. That is not the case. Mindfulness is the awareness of all thoughts. This awareness emerges by paying attention to the present experience without judgment. According to the Cleveland Clinic, an average person has about 60,000 thoughts a day. That is a high number and it is impossible to stop thinking. In order to cultivate mindfulness in one's life, one needs to be aware of only a few of these thoughts without trying to stop thinking.

Practicing that alone qualifies as practicing mindfulness. It is the simplicity of being aware of one's own life as it unfolds, instead of worrying about what is about to come. Mindfulness requires constant practice if one seeks to reap benefits from it. Thankfully, mindfulness does not need a lengthy meditation practice or a yoga class.

Some people become intimidated because they think that mindfulness is something obscure or exotic. It is not. Everyone is actually very familiar to mindfulness because everyone practices it, in a way. Everyone is capable to be present in the moment. All they need to do is cultivate these innate qualities with simple practices.

Mindfulness is something so simple that anyone can do it. It cultivates human qualities that are universal and there is no need to change religion or lifestyle. It is easy to learn. Mindfulness is also a practice that brings awareness and caring into everything people do, not to mention that it cuts needless stress, even the little ones. What makes mindfulness practices a good idea to try out is the fact that there are benefits proven by numerous scientific studies that are positive for health, happiness, relationships, and work. Moreover, when people deal with the world's ever-increasing uncertainty and complexity, mindfulness can pave a way to an effective response to the problem.

As such, we invite you to practice mindfulness whenever you can because the world has many beautiful things to offer, and you could only see them when you stop, clear your mind, and notice them. Stop worrying so much and appreciate the precious things you have. You are the only one who can bring happiness to yourself, so do it now when you still can.

Chapter 5: Improving Social Skills

Of course, calming yourself down will only go so far in social situations. In addition to reducing your anxiety in social situations, you also need to work on your social skills. Let's be honest here. We are only socially anxious because we lack in certain areas of our social skills. That is completely fine. We all have to start somewhere, and you can always work on it. The previous chapter is intended to help you quell social anxiety if you find yourself in one, unprepared. That or the things you could do to calm yourself before and after you have mingled. This section focuses solely on improving your social skills to be a confident, approachable, and lovable individual so you can achieve your greatest potential.

If you truly wish to overcome social anxiety, you need to improve your social skills so your confidence and self-esteem grow. You need to go back on the offensive instead of staying in the defensive and waiting for social anxiety to happen to you. If you are that anxious about yourself, you know that you need to improve your social skills. That is alright. The first step is always acknowledging the existence of the problem. Let's start from the top, shall we?

Introduction

Setting the right foot forward in any social situation will help you immensely right from the get-go. Introductions are important because they help you get to know people, familiarize yourself with them, and put both you and others at ease. Thankfully, introducing yourself gets easier with practice. There are four simple steps to making introductions.

Who to Whom?

First, determine who should be introduced to whom. The rule of thumb is that you should always say the name of the older or higher-ranking individual first. For instance, in a professional environment, you say something like "Mrs. Smith, I'd like to introduce you to my friend, Jill."

When both sides are equal, you should introduce the name of the person whom you know better first. In a business context, the client is considered to be a higher-ranking individual. At a party, you should introduce guests to the guest of honor.

Other than in a casual setting, always use first and last names, as well as titles such as "Dr." whenever appropriate. If the person that you are introducing has a relationship to you, whatever it may be (tutor, spouse, sibling, parent, classmate, friend, etc.) share this with others.

For example: "Natalie Jones, I'd like you to meet Jonah Edberg." (Natalie is older than Jonah)

"Mister President, I'd like to introduce my friend Paul." (the President is a higher-ranking individual)

In a group setting like in a party, always introduce a person to the group first. For instance, "Jake, these are my friends Elizabeth, Jill, Steve, and Natasha. Everyone, this is David." A rule of thumb here is that you should apply this introduction technique when you need to introduce to a group of up to six people. If there are more than that, it is best to only introduce that person to those that are nearby or those that the person will be sitting with. Leading someone around the room making introductions is a bad idea and should be avoided at all costs.

Another rule is that when you are introduced to someone, it is polite to say "How are you?" If you are introduced to someone that you have been told about, you can say something like "-Name- has told me so much about you!"

What if someone has forgotten to introduce you? This is your time to go on and introduce yourself and explain how you know the host if you are at a party. In a business setting, it is better if you are the one to extend your hand for a handshake if you are the higher-ranking individual in the pair. It is also better to just wait after the introduction to shake hands, so you can concentrate on the person's name first.

There are also other things you should consider:

- If you forgot someone's name, it is actually politer and less awkward if you just openly acknowledge the fact that to avoid an introduction altogether. Just say something like, "I'm sorry/I do apologize, but I seem to have forgotten your name." The other person has been in your position before. They will almost certainly not hold a grudge against you.
- If you are being introduced to a group of people, there is no need to say something after each introduction. It is fine to just nod after the first introduction so you do not have to repeat yourself. If anything, repeating yourself is more awkward than nodding.

- Formal etiquette rules say that men should stand when being introduced to women. Women should stand when being introduced to older women. However, be aware of the situation and actions of those around you when you are deciding whether to stand up.
- There is no rush in making an introduction. Make sure you speak slowly so everyone can understand the names you are saying.
- While you should use people's titles when you introduce them, you should not use titles when you introduce yourself. They will make you sound stuffy.
- According to a 2012 study of 30 socially anxious individual and 30 low socially anxious individuals, it is found that socially anxious individuals feel less anxious when they had a brief internet chat with the stranger before meeting them. Therefore, the study authors proposed that computer-medication communication (CMC) could be a useful form of safety behaviors as socially

anxious individuals can be themselves and disconfirm negative beliefs. Therefore, if you chat with someone a bit online before meeting them, you have a higher chance of overcoming negative thoughts when you first meet someone in person. Instead of thinking of how nervous you are, you might think of the fact that you had a good chat online and that the other person has quite a few things in common with you. You can then pick things up from there.

Eye Contact

Eye contact anxiety refers to the discomfort about making eye contact or looking at other people in the eye. An individual with eye contact anxiety might feel that they cannot look at other people in the eyes when talking or feel like they are being judged or scrutinized when making eye contact. This can be because of our genetic or lack of practice. If you have a social anxiety disorder, the part of your brain that warns you of danger can be triggered by eye contact. In most cases, though, you just do not have enough practice in making eye contact. This is because of shyness or the fact that, in your culture, making eye contact is considered rude.

According to a 2017 review in Current Psychiatry Reports, social anxiety is related to a combination of being on guard and avoiding processing emotional social stimuli. That means that when you are at a party, you might be on the lookout for people who seem to be judging you. You might also try to avoid the situation in which you feel that you are being judged as well. Moreover, the review showed that socially anxious individuals often avoid maintaining eye contact, which is likely due to the fear of being judged.

With eye contact considered to be something vital for both your career and personal relationships, it is crucial that you learn to develop.While some people might be predisposed to fearing or avoiding eye contact altogether, most people can learn to improve their eye contact skill by becoming better at making good eye contact. Therefore, overcoming eye contact anxiety is a two-part process. First, you need to minimize or eliminate eye contact anxiety and then you can proceed to improve your skills for making eye contact.

Reducing Eye Contact Anxiety

Individuals with an anxiety disorder can benefit from treatments such as cognitive-behavioral therapy or simple medications. Most people with a social anxiety disorder can overcome their fear response and maintain good eye contact with practice, though. Therefore, eye contact is just another aspect of socialization that you can get used to with practice and exposure.

If you have not been diagnosed with an anxiety disorder but still find that eye contact is uncomfortable for you, you can build up your tolerance through exposure by engaging in increasing amounts of eye contact over time.

Eventually, it should feel less uncomfortable for you as you do it more often.

Start by making eye contact with people who do not make you feel as anxious. Practice with your friend or family. From there, work your way up to more anxiety-provoking situations such as your work supervisor. If you are uncomfortable still, you can also try to make eye contact with characters on televisions. You can find YouTube videos just for that purpose as well. If you become more anxious before or during situations when you need to make eye contact, try practicing deep breathing exercise from your diaphragm to slow your heart rate down so to calm yourself.

Improving Eye Contact Skills

If you are talking to someone one-on-one, or when you are looking at people within a group, you can just look at a spot between, or slightly above the listener's eyes, or between their brows. The other person cannot tell if you are actually looking into their eyes. If this is still uncomfortable, try letting your eyes fall out of focus which also relaxes and softens your gaze. Don't forget to look away sometimes because staring too intensely will make people uncomfortable.

Practicing the above will help you make eye contact better and make your listeners feel more connected to you, not to mention that it will make you feel more comfortable when you are speaking either to a group or to a person.

If you are speaking to a group, instead of seeing them as a whole unit, imagine talking to each individual in the group at a time. So, as you speak, select one person in the group and pretend that you are talking to just that person. Look at them as you finish your sentence or idea before moving on to look at another person. Make sure you look at everyone in the group. Of course, if you have a large audience, you can just look at an individual in one general direction before switching to the next one.

There are some other tips to consider:

- The 50/70 rule: maintain eye contact 50% of the time when you speak, and 70% when you listen.
- Eye contacts should last for 4 to 5 seconds at a time, or about as much time as you need to tell the color of their eyes. When you break eye contact, look to the side before resuming your gaze. However, when you break eye contact, do it slowly because looking away too quickly or darting your eyes can make you look nervous or shy. Moreover, do not look down when you look away because this shows a lack of confidence.
- If looking at someone directly in the eyes is uncomfortable for you, you can look at another spot on their face. Think of an inverted triangle connecting their eyes and mouth. Every five seconds or so, switch to a different point of the triangle you are looking at. You can also look at their nose, mouth, or chin.

- When you do break eye contact, make a gesture or nod because this looks more natural than just looking away. The other person might think that you have grown uncomfortable with the amount of eye contact.

Giving Compliments

Socially anxious individuals rarely give compliments not because they do not appreciate what other people do, they just feel awkward and think they would come across as awkward if they do. However, learning how to give good compliments and practicing it every day can enable you to become natural at giving praise. Giving compliments is an important social skill as it is also a great way to start a conversation on the right food, develop social bonds, and reduce anxiety about communicating. Here are nine tips

- Time your compliments well. Never give them out randomly. You should genuinely

believe the compliments or they will come across as fake.
- Be specific with your compliments. Instead of saying, "Your living room looks great!", say something like, "Your living room looks great! I love how the decors spice up the place."
- Just like receiving compliments, giving them help you start a conversation. Using the previous example, you can ask "How did you come up with such a decoration idea?"
- When giving out compliments, consider the setting and your relationship with the person so you can make sure that the compliment is appropriate. Any compliments of a personal nature should be offered to a close friend in a private setting.
- Creative compliments with uncommon words stick around far longer than generic-sounding ones. So, instead of saying "Your

new dress is really nice," say, "Your new dress looks fabulous!"

- Whenever possible, compliment the person's traits rather than their appearance because such compliments are rare. For example, compliment a father for his compassion for his children or a teacher for her ability to keep students motivated.

- Be willing to give constructive criticism on top of giving genuine compliments. Compliments will mean a lot more when the receiver knows that you are not afraid to be open about their own flaws as well.

- Do not be afraid to compliment people in authority because people in power actually receive fewer compliments and your giving them compliments will be a pleasant surprise. You might be surprised to see the good response from them and they will most likely welcome the positive feedback.

- When complimenting someone with low self-esteem, it might be better to compliment their behaviors rather than their personal characteristics. Also, you should avoid inflated praise.

Receiving Compliments

On the flip side, it is a good idea to learn how to receive compliments as well. If you are socially anxious, you know very well how hard it is for you to gracefully accepting compliments. Whenever you receive a compliment, you might be dismissive and downplay the positive attribute. For instance, if your work supervisor tells you how well you did your job, you might respond by saying, "Well, anyone could have done what I did." This kind of response does not help as it only erodes your confidence more. In a way, your response just implies that you do not value your work, your appearance, your home, or whatever it is you receive a compliment about. So, this is how you respond to compliments.

- Say "Thank you". This is enough, even if you cannot think of anything else to say.

Try not to pause too long before saying it though, because your sincerity might come across as questionable.

- If you can come up with one, add a positive comment on top of the compliment, like, "I put a lot of time into this," or, "I took a lot of time choosing the color scheme for this room."
- Whenever possible, return the compliment with a comment, "I really appreciate that coming from you. That means a lot."
- If you want, you can take this one step further by turning it into a conversation starter such as "I've been meaning to ask you how you would have done this differently," or "I actually wanted to ask your opinion about this…"

Example Scenario

Tom is attending a party at his new office. To get ready for the event, he went to the barbershop to get a new, stylish haircut that he had never tried out before. It turned out pretty well and he is actually feeling pretty good about how he looks although he was a bit anxious about the event.

However, when he walked through the door to the office, a fellow colleague greets him and says, "Wow! I love your new hairstyle! You look dashing!" Flattered or embarrassed by the attention he is getting, Tom pauses and eventually says, "You think so? I'm actually not sure if I should keep it this way."

Now, for those with a social anxiety disorder, this situation is not really unrealistic. If you tend to respond negatively to compliments, it will take some practice and dedication to learn a better way to react. So, how could Tom have responded in a more positive way to his colleague's compliment? Something like below would be a much better way to accept the compliment, showing grace to the compliment giver and boosting Tom's self-esteem the same time:

"Thank you! I love the style, too – I just had it done. Coming from you, I really appreciate it. Your hair always looks amazing as well. Which barber do you go to?"

As you can see, the above response combined all four tips from the above. You start with a "thank you", a positive comment, a compliment back to the compliment giver, and a conversation starter. Compliments might be just what you need to get the conversation going. If someone gives you a compliment, that means that they want to get to know you more and will be receptive to conversation opener like the one stated above.

Bad Handshakes

A handshake is one of the first things you do to leave first impressions, and messing it up could potentially ruin everything. It is possible to overcome the initial bad first impression by dressing up well, coming on time, behaving well, etc., it is easier to learn how to avoid some typical handshakes that feel off. Giving a firm grip and a tug is enough, but some people tend to make the following mistakes:

Aggressive Handshakes

These types of handshakes will make you come across as rude or demanding, leaving a sour aftertaste after the shake. They are:

Dominant Handshake

This kind of handshake involves putting your palm downward when you offer your hand, therefore forcing the other person to put theirs facing up in a submissive position. This is a form of aggression. While the dominant handshake is appropriate in certain circumstances, it should be avoided in everyday situations.

If you find that you are on the receiving end of the dominant handshake, there is an easy fix you can make. Just take a step to the left, forcing both hands to naturally straighten.

Bone Crusher

Just like the dominant handshake, the Bone Crusher is very aggressive and involves an excessively strong grip that may cause discomfort or even pain for the recipient. If you have been on the receiving end of it, you know what it feels like. Handshake grip should not be harder than the strength you need to hold the door handle. Moreover, your grip should match that of the other person. Older adults also need a looser grip.

If you ever find yourself on the wrong end of the bone crusher handshake, say something like, "Wow, strong handshake!" Most of the time, the other person will loosen their grip on you.

Double-Handed

Although there are cases when the double-handed handshake is appropriate. If you used this kind of handshake when meeting someone for the first time, it may seem overly personal or intimate. Unless you are a politician or grandmother, it is best if you reserve this kind of handshake for close friends.

Too Close

Just like the dominant handshake or the bone crusher, this handshake involves the other person coming too close to you to shake hands, therefore invading your personal space. That or they pull you in closer to them as you two are shaking hands. Either way, this closeness of the handshake will make the recipient feels uncomfortable. You can fix this problem by simply taking a step back. Unless the other person has you in a vice grip, reclaiming your personal space is relatively easy.

Passive Handshakes

Passive handshakes would make you come off as nervous, uncertain, or otherwise uninvolved or disinterested. Just like aggressive handshakes, these will also hamper your career.

Limp Fish

Limp fish is the opposite of bone crusher. A limp handshake tells the other person that you are disinterested or anxious, which can be detrimental to your career. If you are not sure if your handshake is limp, ask your friend to practice it with you until you master your grip.

Fingers Only

This is a worse variation, which you only offer your fingers to the other person. To avoid this kind of handshake. Be sure that the webbed part of your hand between your pointer finger and thumb is touching the other person's hand before tightening your grip.

Cold, Clammy, or Sweaty

You might give the other person cold, clammy, or even sweaty handshakes in social situations. While it feels that the situation is out of your control, there are ways you can try and lessen the impact.

Make sure to have a paper towel handy to wipe off sweaty palms in secret when you have a chance. Avoid carrying a cold drink in your right hand if you know that you will meet people. If your hands become cold often, warm them up with an instant heat packet in your pocket or a hot air dryer in the restroom first.

No Eye Contact

If you have shaken hands with someone who would not look at you in the eyes, you might have wondered what they had to hide. Not making eye contact during a handshake tells the other person that you are not being open. If your lack of eye contact is because of social anxiety, you can practice using the tricks we have discussed previously. Basically, you can try looking between the person's brows so at least the other person thinks that you are looking into their eyes.

Other Bad Handshakes

This is the awkward kind of handshake that just does not come across properly, not particularly aggressive or passive. They are:

The Miss

This is a handshake that does not come together right. Maybe you want to shake hands but ended up shaking fingers instead. Perhaps you clumsily shook hands and could not wait to pull your hands back. Whatever it is that you did wrong, remember that the other person feels just as responsible for it, and that is accidental.

Long Handshake

Long handshakes, as the name suggests, lasts far longer than it should. Perhaps the other person is still pumping your hands up and down long after introductions are through. The ideal handshake lasts only a few seconds and does not go on longer than the verbal introduction. Any longer than that and it makes you two seem like holding hands, which is awkward.

Being Assertive

People with social anxiety disorder often have trouble being assertive. If you have a social anxiety disorder, it is difficult for you to be upfront with your feelings and sharing them with others is hard, to the point that you would just keep it to yourself. The only problem is that no one can read your mind, so you will often find your needs not being met.

Assertive communication is a straightforward and open expression of your needs, desires, thoughts, and feelings. It involves advocating for your own needs while still taking that of others into consideration. It involves the use of "I" statement, like "I need some help with this project." It is also a way of making sure that your needs are met while still considering that of others.

Communicating assertively will feel uncomfortable at first for you, and you have probably already adopted a passive communication style to avoid conflict. However, this would leave you feeling anxious, depressed, helpless, frustrated, and uncomfortable. It is worth pointing out that communicating assertively is not being selfish. It is actually an effective way of negotiating social encounters. Assertive individuals are not pushy or obnoxious or do they step on others' feelings to get what they want. Assertive communication involves making your feelings, needs, and desires known in a non-threatening and nonjudgmental way. This kind of communication is actually helpful because you make it clear of what you want and others can refuse your requests if your needs conflict with theirs when you do it in a non-threatening way. Being polite and respectful while being assertive pave a way for a healthy discussion and negotiation, leading up to a compromise and a win-win scenario where both parties are happy with what they get as their needs are best met in that scenario.

Still unsure if assertive communication is the best way to go? Think about what would happen if all of your daily encounters are with people who communicate and behave assertively. They will tell you upfront what they need from you while expecting you to refuse if their needs interfere with yours. At the same time, they also expect you to tell them exactly what you need. So, instead of expecting others to read your mind or hoping that they guess what you want, you want to be clear about what your needs. Be honest and open about them.

For example, your work supervisor asks you to work overtime for the day, but you have plans with your family for the evening. She is clear about the fact that the project was urgent and it needs to be completed as soon as possible. You make it clear that you did not have many opportunities to spend quality time with your family. You respect the fact that the project is important to the company. She respects the fact that family is just as important to you. After a brief discussion, she offers you a

Friday off next week to spend with your family instead if you work overtime today. That way, she can still get the project done and you can still spend time with your family. This is the kind of situation assertive communication leads to.

How to Become More Assertive

As previously mentioned, assertive communication normally being with the word "I", and always expresses what you are feeling or thinking. Again, being assertive does not mean stepping on others or berating them. The objective of being assertive is to negotiate to arrive at a compromise that would best benefit everyone. Some examples of assertive statements include:

- I like to watch action films.
- I am disappointed that you talked about me behind my back.
- I know that children come first, but I just feel disheartened that I do not get to spend any time together.
- I enjoyed talking with you.

To speak assertively, put these pieces of the sentence together:

- Start with "I"
- Add a verb to describe your feelings such as: like, dislike, need, feel, love, wish, etc.
- Finish the sentence to express exactly what it is that makes you feel that way.

Remember to leave "you" out of the sentence so the other person does not feel that they are being accused, which would cause them to become defensive. Keep your emotions under control and just openly share what you really feel. So, using the previous example, you will say something like:

- I…
- Can't…
- Stay overnight because I promised to spend time with my family.

It does not look overly complicated, does it? It is simple, and that is what it is all about – being direct and honest with your needs. When you start to do it regularly, it will start to feel more natural. It is important for you to learn how to say no because this is an area where you will struggle if you have social anxiety.

Assertive Nonverbal Behavior

In addition to what you say, your nonverbal communication might also fall under the passive category if you have social anxiety. See if you can tell which one is passive, assertive, or aggressive nonverbal communication.

Example 1: Julie keeps quiet, hoping that everyone will guess what she wants. She speaks with a weak voice and does so hesitantly, not to mention that she gives up easily. She often looks down or away, has poor posture, and keeps her head down. She fidgets a lot and nods all the time, no matter what is said.

Example 2: Jess pays very close attention to what is being said around her, speaks with a strong yet relaxed voice, makes good eye contact, and stands up straight. She makes her concerns clear and always try to seek out fairness in situations.

Example 3: Tom is sarcastic and always comes across like a know-it-all. He needs to win all the time, no matter whether he is actually right or wrong. He speaks loudly, stares at people, stands with his feet apart and hands on his hips, pointing his fingers at everyone and move abruptly.

The second style is the kind of nonverbal behavior you need to go for – that of Jess, which reflects assertive nonverbal behavior.

Getting Over the Fear of Conflict

After some practice, let's say that you know how to speak assertively, verbal and nonverbal. But there is just one problem: you are still afraid of conflict. This is normal. The fear of conflict with others is common even among those who do not have social anxiety. You might be worried about saying something that upsets others or that others will disagree with. Maybe you have general fears about doing the things that might annoy or bother others. While avoiding conflict altogether alleviates your anxiety immediately, it does not help you in the long term. It will perpetuate your fear that you cannot handle situations that involve conflicts. So how do you overcome the fear of conflict?

Exposure Therapy

We already talked about how exposure therapy helps you overcome anxiety by putting yourself in increasingly anxious-provoking situations. The same also works in overcoming the fear of conflict. Exposure therapy is actually a part of a larger treatment program such as cognitive-behavioral therapy. As always, you can always practice exposures on your own by forming a self-help plan. The idea is not to run out to the first people you meet and start an argument. It is quite the contrary. You simply need to gradually immerse yourself fin seared scenarios at a tolerable pace.

So, you start out with a conflict that you feel the least anxious and work your way up to more and more intense conflict until you no longer fear any of them. You can either practice this in real life as opportunities present themselves or in your imagination. The second option has an added benefit of helping you plan out exactly what you want to say when you are confronted with such a situation because you can envision the exact scenario that causes you to fear when you cannot construct it in real life. However, the first one gives you the real-world experience that you need. As such, it is worth practicing both.

How to Practice It Safely

Envisioning a conflict situation should be the first step as you are in control of the whole situation without threatening you in any way. Conflicts often happen, but it is outside your control so you will never know when. It is hard to be prepared for something that happens spontaneously, so you might have a lack of practice when it comes to actually resolve a conflict assertively. Moreover, unlike other exposures, exposure therapy involving conflict with others has the potential to cause others to be irritated, irate, or impatient. So, approach every situation using assertive behavior rather than aggressive behaviors, and choose to engage in situations where there is little risk. For instance, do not practice exposures with someone who is easily agitated or your own work supervisor.

Remember that the entire point of this exposure therapy is to increase your ability to tolerate conflict, and you may inconvenience others in the process. While the fact that you may feel terrible for what you are doing is laudable, others will most likely see it as a minor issue even those who are on the receiving end. After all, conflict happens all the time. Think about how you would feel or react if such things happen to you. Most of the time, you would be bothered temporarily, but you would quickly forget about it.

Fear Hierarchy

Just like making a list of social situations that make you feel anxious, you need to make a list of scenarios that would cause conflict, starting with the easiest task and work your way up to the hardest. Here are some ideas:

- Take longer to do something: Take your time to parallel park. Be indecisive when a salesperson is helping you. Take more time when using an ATM. Use multiple coupons at the grocery store and ask them to do a price match.
- Say no: Ask the telemarketer to put you on the "do not call" list, say no to a friend who asks too much from you, refuse to do more than your share of the work when a coworker asks you to do theirs.
- Return something or complain about something: Return an item to the store without the receipt, tell a server after your meal that the service was too slow, tell the

hairdresser that you are not very happy with your haircut and ask for a change. Of course, make sure that your complaints are valid so you can convey them realistically.

- Create a problem: Buy more than you have money to pay for, pretend to realize that at the checkout, so you have to put an item back. Take an item that does not have a price tag to the cashier. Try to pay with a debit card that you know will bounce.
- Ask someone to stop doing something: Say something assertive when someone cuts in front of you in line. Stand up for someone who is being bullied. Tell someone politely that you disagree with their opinion.

Dealing with Neighbors

If you are suffering from social anxiety disorder, you will find it hard to interact with your neighbor. In fact, dealing with your neighbor is probably one of the things in your list of exposure for both assertive communication practices and social interaction. Have you ever experience that time when you are about to leave your apartment, but heard that your neighbor is in the hallway and you suddenly convinced yourself that you need to stay in for a bit longer to do "some important things"? You may avoid talking to your neighbors or time your entrance or exit so that you do not have to talk to them. Over time, such avoidance strategies will come back to bite you in the ankle, leaving you a prisoner in your own home.

It will be hard for you at first to get to know your neighbor, but doing so has many benefits. Knowing those who live around you makes the neighborhood or apartment safer. Plus, they can help you out sometimes and you might even find them a good friend. Being friendly with your neighbor does not have to be hard. There are a few things you need to know to get started:

- If you are the new neighbor in the area, try your best to make a good impression. Choose a time to introduce yourself when your neighbor seems relaxed and not in a hurry. Wave, smile and go to them to introduce yourself. You can talk a little bit with them such as the area that you live in, activities, and things to do in town.

- When you see your neighbor again, take the time to have a chit-chat if they are interested in talking. If you are not sure what to say, find something you can compliment, such as their yard.
- If you are feeling more confident about yourself and your neighbor seems to have quite a few things in common with you and you want to get to know them better, create a reason to talk to them again. Go over to their place to borrow an item for a recipe or a tool for a project. If you borrow an ingredient, invite them over to have a sample of what you are making when it is done. Maybe even give them some of the stuff you make. That way, you have more things to talk about.

- If you have little in common with your neighbors, a simple wave and hello whenever you see each other is all that is needed, especially if you see that friendship is going nowhere.

Starting Conversations

To some, starting a conversation with a stranger is a piece of cake. For those with social anxiety, though, that is a completely different story. A room full of strangers can be frightening. If you are looking to start a conversation with an authority figure, then you will most likely feel more anxious.

In reality, starting a conversation is very simple. Focus on the other person or say something light-hearted. You just need to make an introductory statement. What you say is not as important as long as the other person as the chance to say something else.

Comment on Something Personal

Most of the time, the person that you are trying to start a conversation with will have something unique about themselves. Maybe it is an exquisite piece of jewelry, a beautiful shirt, or maybe a tattoo. Anything works as long as it is distinctive that tells a story about the person so you can start a conversation about it. Say something like:

- That shirt looks really nice. Where did you buy it?
- Is that a tattoo of Groot on your arm?
- That is a really beautiful watch. Which brand is it?

Of course, you should not start with anything too intimate or you will probably offend the other person. You should not ask them about whether their hair color is real or if they are a regular at the gym. After you get your response, think of something to create a common platform to build a conversation and relationship upon. So, before you start commenting, think of a follow-up story right away. This is the key to a conversation. Here, you need to follow up with something somewhat personal that is related to the other person and tell them something interesting about you. Using the above example, we have:

- The only place I've seen a shirt that lovely was at a bazaar in China.
- I love tattoos and I've been thinking of getting one myself. But I'm not sure what to get. How did you decide on Groot?
- I've seen many businessmen wearing them. Is there a reason why?

These statements help you connect with the other person and keep the conversation going. Again, the point here is not about saying all the right things or coming across a certain way. It is all about getting the conversation going.

"Haven't I Seen You Somewhere Before?"

Under the right circumstances, this conversation opener might work very well. If you say, "You seem really familiar, do I know you from somewhere?" to a person, it will make it a lot easier for you to gather information about the other person and start a conversation. Here are a few ideas:

- I've been to that Starbucks.
- Where do you work?
- I was in the band, did you play an instrument?
- What high-school did you attend?

When you go through the details of the other person's life story, you can go on to other topics. Again, the idea is to not find out whether you have met that other person before. Chances are you have not. You just need to get to know the other person.

Make a Funny Comment

This is perhaps one of the best ways to start a conversation because it starts off on a light-hearted tone. So, make a funny comment about your surroundings such as:

- Do you think our lecturer looks like Harry Potter?
- Wait, is that guy sleeping at the front row?

Remember, when making jokes, you should never want it to be mean-spirited or judgmental. Make sure your comments are positive. From there, try to invite others in on the joke. Using the previous example, we have:

- Where do you think he keeps his wand?
- Do you think the lecturer will notice?

Remember that this kind of conversation is risky though. Humor is tricky when you use it on someone that you do not know well. However, if the other person shares your sense of humor, then you might have started a great friendship. Think of this as testing the water, to find if the other person thinks the way you do.

Because this kind of conversation starter is risky, remember that it is likely to fail some of the time. If you do not receive a positive response, remember that there are always other people you can approach. If you are persistent enough, it will get easier for you to talk to strangers. When you become more confident and comfortable, you do not need to rely on such tricks to start conversations.

Joining Conversations

The ability to join conversations spontaneously and smoothly is a key social skill. If you need to join in a conversation at a party or gathering with people with whom you do not know very well, being able to slide in the conversation with a group or individual will make you feel included, not to mention giving you a chance of making new friends. Here are some ideas you can implement so you can slide in there smoothly:

Prepare Topics for Conversation

Before you even attempt to join a conversation, do some reading so you can be informed and can share your opinions. Read the news, follow popular topics, or at the very least, be aware of any current events that are likely to come up in conversations. These will help you when you join a conversation. Not only that you have something to refer to for what is being discussed, but you might also even be able to add another perspective or share something unique with the group like talking about your travel experience or favorite author.

Choose a Group

Different groups of people will have different things to talk about, so choose a group of people who are in a conversation with a topic you want to join in. It is also a good idea to join in a group with someone you already know, or a group that is talking about something that you know or are interested in. However, just like anything in life, you do not need to look for that perfect group. Any will do as long as you can practice entering into conversations that are already ongoing. You do not need to have the world's best conversation.

Listen and Make Eye Contact

Remain on the edge of the group while they are talking and listen in to know what they are talking about. From there, make eye contact with one or two people in the group to show that you are also interested in what is being discussed. Socially anxious might seem aloof or standoffish if they do not make eye contact, so try your best to look at people in the eye as you talk to put others at ease.

Be Polite

There are a time and place for everything, and the same applies to conversations participation. Wait for a natural break in the conversation before you speak. Instead of jumping into the conversation as a person is talking, politely acknowledge that you are just joining in the talk, wait for a pause, and say something like, "Are you talking about last night's accident?" or "Can I ask a question?"

Show Interest

Be genuinely interested in what the other person has to say, or at least show that you are. Listen very carefully and reflect back on what you have heard. Ask open-ended questions so that others are encouraged to speak and share their opinions. Asking close-ended questions would lead to an awkward silence as the answers would be short and do not contribute to the conversation at all unless you follow it up with an open-ended question.

Because socially anxious people have trouble holding up their end of the conversation, it is crucial that you try your very best to be receptive to what others say, especially when you join in a new group.

Think of it this way Would you rather be talking to someone who is open, warm and friendly, or someone who is fearful, closed off, and cold? Be the person that you want to talk to and others will want to talk to you more often.

Practice

Now that we have covered the basics, all you need to do is to implement all of these tips into practice. Look for opportunities to join in conversations. You used to back away from a group conversation in the past, so try to join it just to practice. Use the acronym "CLASS" to remember the tips above:

- **C**hoose a group
- **L**isten
- **A**sk questions
- **S**how interest
- **S**hare your ideas

Next time when you see a group you want to join, remember the CLASS acronym and you should have a clear idea on how to join a group conversation. If you find yourself in a group of people but cannot bring yourself to talk, then you might need to purposely put yourself in a position that requires you to talk to others. For example, you might volunteer to be the group leader for that project. This new role will force you out of your comfort zone and engage in dialogues that you need, especially if you are the type of person who wants to get a job done well. Just take breaks from time to time if it tires you. Eventually, you will feel better in engaging in conversations.

Small Talk Ideas

Small talks are one of the things that people with social anxiety avoid like the plague. These are the best source of conversation between people who do not know each other well. As such, learning to make small talk can strengthen your confidence so you can start conversations, make connections, and improve your social skills.

A good way to alleviate anxiety is to prepare for the types of topics that you know will most likely be talked about. It takes more than knowing what to say to make small talks. You also need to know what is best to keep private. Moreover, it is just as important to overcome your urge to avoid small talks altogether. Rather than being afraid of small talks, try your best to overcome your fear of it. So, here are some of the best and worst ideas for small talks and why:

Good Topics

The general rule is that it is something popular that you know the other person is interested in and can understand, or something that is general enough that allows you to talk about it for a moment before moving on to other, more serious topics. They are:

Weather

Although talking about the weather seems like a really boring, if not a lazy idea, it is a neutral topic that anyone can discuss. Are you in the middle of a heatwave? Did a big storm just blow through? It is really cloudy today? Look outside your door and you have some good conversation openers. You can say something like:

- "Lovely day, isn't it?"
- "Looks like it's gonna rain…"

Practice making small talk about the weather by asking them such questions will help prevent an awkward silence.

Arts and Entertainment

This works especially well after the release of a new movie, popular music, books, restaurants, television shows, etc. To prepare for these topics though, you need to catch up with the current trends. You need to know what is popular and always be in the middle of reading a good book or something to that effect. That way, you can ask someone, "Have you seen any good movies lately?" Now, you might need to ask about ten people before you get someone interested in talking to you. That is okay because you also need to learn how to cope with rejection, so you might need to seek it out. It's all about practice, nothing else.

Sports

You can discuss your favorite teams, sporting events, tournaments, or even bowl games. Just like the above, you need to keep track of what sports are played during which season like soccer, football, hockey, or golf, so you are always up-to-date with the current even. If the Olympics are taking place, everyone will be talking about it all the time. If you don't like sports, you can always talk about why you don't like them.

You can start a conversation by asking something like, "Did you catch that golf tournament on the weekend?" This will be uncomfortable the first few times, but it will eventually feel more natural to you.

News

Another way to kick-start a small talk is to read the news daily and talk about them. Be aware of what is going on in the world and in your city. Newspapers are out of style, and you can always get your dose via digital news directly from the news website or social media. Here are a few conversation starters:

- What do you think about the workers going on strike?
- I read that they are bumping up the gas price, did you hear about that?
- Did you hear about the new amusement park they are building?

Remember that small talk is intended to build a bridge to connect you to another person. What you two are going to talk about is not really important from here. What matters is that you start talking.

Family

People tend to ask you about your family, especially if they know you well or are starting to get to know you. Here, conversation openers include:

- Do you have any siblings?
- Do you have any children?

- How long have you been married?

At the same time, you also need to be prepared for the same types of question by asking others about their families. This sort of small talks shows your communication skills while also allowing you to learn more about the person in a short period of time.

Work

Yet another common small topic is work. Someone may ask you what do you do for a living, or whether you like your job. If your line of work is something unusual and hard to explain, consider keeping business cards in your wallet. This works well if your company or job has a website that people can visit to learn more. Here, conversation openers include:

- Do you like your job?
- How long have you worked there?
- That is an intriguing line of work. How did you get into it?

Only focus on what you want to learn about others and the things you enjoy talking about, though. This makes the small talk more like a fun-filled activity than a chore.

Travel

Everyone loves to talk about their vacations. If you travel anywhere, be prepared to answer questions and give opinions about all the places you have visited and the activities you have done there. It is a good idea to put together a vacation album so you can show people who visit your home.

While you are at that, why not ask others about their favorite travel destinations? Ask what they would recommend. Many people are more than happy to share their experience and give you a helping hand.

Celebrity Gossip

Let's get this out of the door: gossiping is not something you should be doing. However, it is a different case with a celebrity because bad publicity is still publicity. You do not have to follow celebrity gossip to make small talks. Still, it isn't a bad idea to know a little bit about some of the most popular celebrities whenever the topic comes up though.

You should save this type of small talk for informal occasions like casual parties. Unless everyone at the workplace is talking about a celebrity, it is better to just lead with something else.

Hobbies

Many people are always willing to talk about their hobbies, and they might be interested in yours. If you do not have a hobby yet, consider taking on something new. Not only that you will have something to talk about, having a hobby gives you a chance to meet others with similar interests.

Just make sure to ask follow-up questions as the other person talks about their hobbies. Listen between the lines as well. If they say, "That was the last time I went diving," ask why.

Hometown

Someone may ask about your hometown as well. For instance:

- What is it like living there?
- Why did you leave?

As always, reciprocate and ask about their hometown as well. You might be surprised to find that someone is from the same place as you, which is a way to form a connection. Have an interesting anecdote or story to tell ready because others will ask you about it as well.

Bad Topics

While the above discusses simple, easy conversation topics that you can use, this section covers the topics that you should avoid at all costs.

Politics

The issue with discussing politics is that someone you are talking to might have very strong opinions. So you can find yourself in the middle of a heated conversation very quickly if you are not careful. It is, therefore, best to just stay away from this topic altogether.

Religion

Just like politics, some people feel very strongly about religion. It is an extremely and potentially sensitive topic that you should avoid.

Sex Life

Talking about it or asking about anything of an intimate nature is inappropriate during small talks. When you talk with strangers, avoid talking about sex or making sexual innuendos because you will make others uncomfortable.

Death

Death is a heavy and emotional topic, which will always dampen the mood of others. So, avoid talking about it during small talks. When you are with strangers, do not talk about any emotional topics that can be upsetting to others.

Age/Appearance

Unless you are talking to someone you know very well, avoid talking about age and appearance. Never ask for a person's age. While it sounds simple and insignificant to you, it can be a hot topic for others. Moreover, do not talk about appearance. Do not ask a woman if she is pregnant or give comments that someone has lost weight. You will never know the reason behind their weight gain or loss. Such topics will produce an awkward situation.

Personal Gossip

Again, gossiping is bad. Celebrity gossip is fair game during small talks, but gossip about other people you know is not. It puts you in a bad light and you will never know if the person you are talking to knows the person being gossiped. So, avoid bad-mouthing others.

Offensive Jokes

Just like gossiping, sensitive jokes should only be shared with your best friends. Better yet, just don't tell them altogether and use jokes that do not have time and place restrictions. Making sexist or racist jokes is offensive and will quickly put you in a bad light, ending your conversation with strangers abruptly.

Narrow Topics

You should also avoid talking about topics that are one-sided. If the other person has not seen the movie, you should not talk at length about the plot or funny scenes because they will have no idea what you are talking about anyway. Watch for signs that they are no longer interested in the topic and find a quick way to end your story.

Past Relationship

On your first date, you should never talk about your past relationship. Making comparisons or talking endlessly about your past love will discourage others and it will just ensure that you will not get a second date.

Leaving a Conversation

Now that you already know how to start, and join a conversation, let us talk about how you could leave a conversation gracefully so you can cover all of your bases. People with social anxiety sometimes have problems leaving conversations. They may leave abruptly because of their high anxiety, they may stay in there far longer than they should because they do not know how to excuse themselves, or they feel anxious in general about the etiquette involved in leaving a conversation.

Knowing how to leave a conversation is just as important as knowing how to leave one. If anything, joining a conversation is actually easier than leaving one for socially anxious individuals. There are a few reasons why you want to leave a conversation such as wanting to excuse yourself to talk to others, wanting to get away from someone who is rude, needing to use the restroom or move on to do other things, or wanting to gracefully end a conversation that is already going nowhere.

You may find yourself in a conversation at work or school settings, parties, casual gatherings, chance meetings with one of your acquaintances, or via telephone conversations. Let us discuss how you could leave a conversation smoothly without it feeling abrupt and awkward:

- Physically distance yourself from the group or person first. Turn yourself a bit away from the person and pull back slowly while still listening to what is being said. Stand up if you were sitting down, and begin using shorter responses to what is being said. The other person will eventually catch on to the fact that you would like to leave the conversation.
- Then, wait for the natural pause in the conversation and then give your reason for leaving. Tell the other person that you need to go to the bathroom or get another drink if you do not have any other reason to give.

Here, it is worth stressing that you do not need to go into the details and explain yourself.

- If possible, an easier transition into leaving involve summarizing that is just being said before mentioning the fact that you are leaving. For instance, you could say, "Sounds like you had a lovely vacation. I'd love to hear more about it. Maybe I might consider going there later. But right now, I have a deadline looming and need to get back to work. Talk to you soon."
- Finally, turn and leave. There is no need to wait for the other person's permission. As you leave, do not look back.

What to Say

So that you have the basics down, you might be unsure of what to say to close the conversation. That is alright. We've got you covered. Here are some examples of what you could say to end a conversation:

- I need to get going, but it's been nice talking to you.
- Well, I'll let you get back to your work. Take care!
- It's been fun chatting with you. I'm going to find Dave before he leaves.
- Thanks for the chat. Talk to you later. (This one works while speaking on the phone)
- I'm just going to excuse myself to use the restroom. Perhaps we can talk later?

Remember, wait for that natural pause.

Other Tips

- Most importantly, do not feel bad about leaving a conversation. Remember that it will end eventually so someone as to do it. If done right, there will be no hurt feelings.
- In a business setting, make plans about when you will be in contact again if appropriate and shake hands before you leave.

- If you want to disengage from the conversation because of what is being said, why not take charge of the conversation yourself? Other people in the group may feel just as uncomfortable and may be looking for someone to change the topic. To do that, just ask questions that branch out to other areas of the conversation.
- As a rule of thumb, it helps if you have an idea of how long do you want to remain in the conversation. Talking with your best friends can last for hours, but conversations with strangers usually last less than 10 minutes. Again, do not feel bad about moving on.
- If you really are stuck in a one-on-one conversation with someone who talks all the time, consider introducing them to another person and hope that both of them hit it off.
- Finally, remember that it is okay to fade back sometimes. You can just leave a conversation quietly without saying

anything, which works well in a group setting with a large number of people.

Dealing with Awkward Conversations

While awkward conversations may seem difficult, they can actually be a good way to practice making small talks and handling conflict, especially if you have a social anxiety disorder. There are a few things you can do to learn to cope with awkward conversations such as planning ahead, brushing up on your soft skills, and knowing when to use humor to lighten up the mood. Awkward conversations can be nerve-wracking to socially anxious individuals, so learning how to cope with awkward conversation will be immensely helpful.

Understand the Awkwardness

First, you need to manage the situation by identifying and understanding the cause of your discomfort. Maybe there are a lot of awkward silences during the conversation or the other person has a strong opinion different from yours, and arguing about it would lead to a heated argument. You need to identify the source of the awkwardness first before you can start figuring out how to solve the problem. If the other person said something that shocked you, it is alright to say something like, "Hold on a minute. I'm just thinking about what you just said," so you can allow yourself some time to process the information without it being awkward.

Keep the Conversation Going

According to a 2010 study from the University of Groningen in the Netherlands called the Experimental Social Psychology Research, fluent conversations lead to self-esteem, social validation, and belonging to a group. So long silences strip you of those feelings, making Journal you feel uncomfortable. So, do your very best to keep the conversation going and both you and the other person will feel more at ease. A good conversation is just like a functional band where everyone is making noises together rather than finding the perfect conversation topic.

Find the Humor

If the conversation feels awkward or otherwise uncomfortable, try doing something to lighten up the mood. The best way to do that is by telling a funny joke or story, poking fun at yourself, or finding the humor in the current situation. It helps break the tension and move the conversation forward if you keep the mood light. Plus, if you are in a group conversation, people will secretly thank you for that.

Agree to Compromise

Sometimes, conversations are awkward because of disagreements. If that is the case, try to find a compromise. Practice empathy toward the other person and try to understand their point of view. Doing so might allow you to understand and accept the perspective of the other person without having to change your own. After all, everything in life is always a different shade of grey, so just because they do not agree with you does not mean that they are completely wrong.

Listen and Paraphrase

If you do not know how what you should say in a conversation, try to reflect back on what you hear and paraphrase what is being said. For instance, if a new friend of yours at university is upset about their poor grades, say something like, "Sounds like you really are upset about your grades this semester…" Doing so tells the other person that you are listening and you sympathize with them. Most of the time, people just want to share their feelings with others. They do not necessarily need a solution, unless they say that out loud. Sometimes, they already know what they should do, but they just want to get their unpleasant feelings out of their chest. Plus, when you do this, it also relieves you of the pressure of trying to come up with what to say next. After all, such topics dampen the mood and can kill a conversation very quickly.

Ask Questions

Maybe you found yourself in a conversation that is awkward because you do not know the other person very well. If that is the case, consider asking questions to try and find a mutual interest that can turn into conversations.

If you know that you will be talking to strangers, try to plan ahead and come up with at least three open-ended questions. They should start with "how" or "what", and you can use this to steer awkward conversations in a more favorable direction. There is no need to be elaborate with your line of questioning, either. Keep it simple like, "So, what's keeping you busy these days?" is more than enough.

You can also ask questions to dig deeper into a topic that was previously discussed in a conversation, or to clarify misunderstandings, and to show that you are paying attention. Just make sure not to ask too many questions consecutively, or they may see you as an interrogator.

Provide a New Topic

Offering a new topic is perfect when the conversation is going nowhere and you feel that the steam is running out. Just like your questions, make sure to have a few topics ready so you can use them when you sense that no one else has anything interesting to say. Some examples include popular TV shows, movies, books, or something that everyone has in common. If you are having a conversation with a group of students, you can talk about the upcoming test at school. If you are talking to your coworkers, you can discuss their next vacation plan. Talking about current events is a common topic that applies to all groups of people. Just make sure that the topic you introduce appeals to your partners.

You can also use the ideas we have discussed earlier about making small talks with strangers. Even mundane topics like the weather isa good place to start. If you want to, you can do some homework to find out the kind of person you will meet and prepare some questions that suit their interests. Alternatively, you can offer them genuine compliments, which we have already discussed), which is also a good way to get the ball rolling.

Be Assertive

If you find yourself talking to a rude individual, who has asked you something inappropriate or just makes you uncomfortable, you must stand up for yourself. Take control by saying something assertive like, "I'd rather not talk about that." Sometimes, you may need to steer the conversation toward a new topic, or you need to outright talk to the other person. You should not keep uncomfortable feelings to yourself or you would otherwise risk ending up feeling resentful and bitter.

Exit Gracefully

If there really is nothing else to say, or you have your own reasons to leave that conversation, be prepared to do it and leave smoothly. Again, we already talked about this. But in short, thank the other person for taking the time to talk, give a reason (it does not have to be elaborate or good), and walk away. If the other person is monopolizing your time and will not let you end the conversation, use an excuse. In a party, you can say that you need to get a drink. In most situations, simply say that you need to use the bathroom.

Keep Quiet

Sometimes, you should not talk at all. Okay, we already said that fluent conversation leads to pleasant feelings of belongings and such, but if you find yourself in a public setting with strangers, talking is not always needed. You may not even need to employ our tactics above about leaving conversations. For instance, the person sitting next to you on the bus or plane may not be interested in talking for the whole trip. That is perfectly fine, and that is something to be expected. If the other person shows signs of disinterest such as giving one-word responses, folds their arms, or leans away, then perhaps you should just let the conversation die quietly.

Making Friends

If you are shy or have social anxiety, you will find it easier to just spend time alone instead of making friends. However, several studies show that people with close friends have a longer life expectancy, and are generally healthier. Moreover, those with close friends can cope with tragedies better such as the death of a loved one or other major life change. You may want to make friends, but the problem is that you do not know how. Some people make it look too easy but you find it to be actually very difficult. Here, we will walk you through the process so you can increase your social circle and hopefully make good friends along the way.

- Remember that before you can attempt to make new friends, you need to take some time to work on yourself first. The more well-rounded a person you are, the higher the chance for you to get along with others. To do this, keep up to date with current events, take up new hobbies, anything you can to do become more comfortable with yourself. This will allow you to make friends easier in those activities. For example, if you are taking guitar classes, you will find people who are also into music. Find out what you are passionate about and seek out like-minded people in the right environment.

- From there, you can start finding potential friends. The best place to start looking for them is also the easiest. Do you work with many people? Do you know someone who has a large circle of friends? Could you join a group or organization so you can be in contact with a larger number of people? You should be too picky in the beginning. After all, anyone could be a potential friend, so first impressions do not tell you the whole story about that person. You need to get to know them first before you can decide whether they could become a long-term friend. So, consider asking a colleague out for lunch, joining a book club at the library, or volunteering at a local non-profit so you can increase your chance of meeting new people and potential friends.

- Moreover, you also need a way to reach out to them and talk. Therefore, make sure that you get their contact information such as their phone number or social media page.
- The most important step in making friends is both accepting invitations and making plans with others. Do your very best to accept any invitations and make the effort to show up. If you turn people down enough times, they will stop asking you to do things. Of course, you should also not expect the other person to make plans. While planning may be a difficult task for people with social anxiety, it is crucial that

you get involved so that others see that you are interested and want to get together.
- When you have begun to form friendships, you need to maintain it by staying in touch. Over time, you will learn how often certain people do that, but make sure you do your part and contact your new friends and make plans. Thanks to online communication, it is not as hard to stay in touch anymore so there is no reason why you cannot keep in touch with those that you meet.

Other Tips

- Building friendship is an ongoing commitment that takes time, effort, and sacrifice. Do not expect instant results. While you make creating new friends a priority, remember that friendship is something to nurture, not just get it and leave it. It does not thrive that way.
- After making new friends, you should never take them for granted. Make your friendship

a priority even when it is the least convenient thing for you right now.
- As a good friend, you should not criticize, gossip, or judge each other.
- Finally, while making friends is important to you, you should never compromise your beliefs, values, or morals just to make a few new friends. If they are different from you in those regards and force you to change those aspects of your life, then they are not your friends. Look for better people elsewhere.

How to Listen Actively

We have talked about how you should listen to others and show genuine interest. This is basically active listening. According to a study back in 2011, it was found that active listening was primarily associated with verbal social skills rather than nonverbal skills. This suggests that being an active listener has more to do with being an effective listener than being able to regulate your nonverbal and emotional communication. So, what does this mean if you live with social anxiety?

Well, active and empathic listens are good at initiating and maintaining conversations, which are two of the most important skills you need to overcome your social anxiety. Plus, when you develop your listening skills, you also improve your conversational ability, but you should not expect that to help you feel any less anxious. You need to address your anxiety separately, but you will have a great time socializing when you addressed your social anxiety and improve your social skills.

Active listening serves the purpose of earning the trust of those around you, helping you understand their situations. Being an active listener also allows you to be assertive because you can only fully understand the other person's needs if you listen carefully and read between the lines. Active listening involves a genuine will to offer support and empathy to the speaker. It is different from critical listening because you are not evaluating the message of the other person so you can offer your own opinion. Instead, active listening is intended to make the speaker feels heard, and maybe solve their problems if they ask for it. The following tips will help you become a better listener:

- Make eye contact as the other person speaks, so they know that you are listening. As a rule, you should look at people in the eyes 60% to 70% of the time. While you do that, lean toward the person, nod your head occasionally, and do not fold your arms or slouch. If you are nervous about looking at people straight in the eyes, look between their brows. They cannot tell the difference.

- Most of the time, the speaker talks to you about their problems or anything about them because they want to be heard. They do not really want to be offered advice or opinions unless they asked for it. So, instead of offering unsolicited opinions or advice, just paraphrase what has been said. You can say something like, "So basically, what you are saying is…" And they will either confirm or deny it and continue talking.

- Do not interrupt the speaker as they are speaking. You should not think of a reply in your head as they speak, either. The last thing the speaker said may change the meaning of what is already said. So, fully focus on the speaker and listen.
- As they speak, try to pick up some nonverbal cues. Sometimes, what they say is not what they really mean. Sometimes, there is a hidden meaning. Look out for facial expressions, tone of voice, and other behaviors as they can tell you more than words alone.
- As you listen, shut down your internal dialogue. Your objective is to fully focus on the speaker, so avoid daydreaming or distractions. It is impossible to attentively listen to someone and your internal voice at the same time.

- Ask questions to clarify what is said. Here, you should ask open-ended questions to encourage the speaker to say more. If they say that they had a great vacation, ask how. Asking closed yes-or-no questions will end conversations very quickly.
- If you are discussing an uncomfortable topic and you want to change it, avoid abruptly changing the subject. It will make you appear that you were not listening at all.
- As you listen, be open, neutral, and withhold your judgment and stereotypes. You do not know the other person, and they are not what you think most of the time.
- Be patient, because we can listen a lot faster than we speak.

If you see that the other person is not being an active listener because they are distracted or disinterested, there are a few things you can do:

- Find a topic that interests you both: This works well during small talks when you try to get to know one another.
- Flip the script: If they are not a good listener, show them how to be one by letting them speak instead. That way, you might help that person learn how to become a better listener.
- Leave: If it is clear that the other person is just not interested in talking to you, or that they are only interested in hearing themselves speak, then it is okay to just walk away.

Chapter 6: Conclusion

In the back of our head, we all worry about so many things – our health, career, life, the suffering,and death of loved ones. When such fears come up, our friends or those we love tend to encourage us out of kindness to think of the best-case scenario. While one might argue that it is a well-meaning move, it can also leave our fears to fester. Leaving our fears unaddressed will fill us with unnamed dread and they might loom far larger than they should. Sometimes, you need to take a brave stance and do the exact opposite. Look at your anxiety in the eye, refuse to be shaken by it, and examine it in exhaustive details so to limit their negative impact on our mind. Doing so will lead all of us to one realization: we could cope, even when the worst came to the worst.

Think about it. If you are worried about your financial situation and how you would lose your friends, then think of what the worse that could happen. Sure, you would have far fewer friends, but those who remain would be your true friends who could see you past your ruined social status to the genuine you beneath. You would perhaps be thrown upon the mercy and charity of others, but you would learn the meaning of true love that is kindness given freely without expecting anything in return.

If you are worried about your social status going to ruins, remember that if that even happens, then it would no longer be an option to follow the safe, respectable, and prestigious path. That does not sound all that bad when you think that, by then, you would have far less to lose and you would then have an opportunity to explore the riskier, but more fulfilling occupations that you wanted but initially been too socially anxious to try. You would know the feeling of inner freedom within those who have stopped trying to be respectable. You would then realize that there is not only one right path and one way things should be. You would realize that the rule-book you had in your mind is useless, and you would learn to make other plans.

If you are worried about rejection, remember that should that happen, you would learn to measure your own self-worth by your own standards rather than the whims and applause of others. You would then develop a sense of self, independent from the thoughts of others. Your failures would then embolden others to share their own stories of sadness, confusion, and humiliation, and everyone would face up to the suffering together which they often unfairly endure alone. You might develop appropriate gratitude for every little thing and every day that unfolds without further tragedy would be recognized and appreciated as the blessing they truly are. You would learn to distinguish between what is very serious and worth lamenting and what is only a nuisance, which would infinitely make you calmer.

If you are worried about your imperfect life, remember that you would learn to look at new admiration and humility at the unhurried calm and natural stoicism and resilience of animals. You would then learn to contemplate your own sorrows from the objective vantagepoint of a distant star and would realize that your life is as petty and insignificant it has always been, so there is no way you could mess up that badly. You would then understand that life is not something that could be shaped into a flawless entity. It would always be imperfect, full of blemishes and imperfection, but it possesses its own beauty and dignity.

If you are worried about the world falling apart all around you, remember that even if it happens, you would see that the struggle for fame, money, and success is only a failed attempt to compensate for an unconditional love that we have always hankered for. You would realize that worldly craving would only lead to melancholy and mourning. You would discover that life is only worthwhile when you live it intensely and gratefully. You might stop to be so scared of looking inside yourself, and might psychotherapy a go. Perhaps you would play the saddest song that you have in your library, waiting for you all this time. You might retreat to bed under your covers,cry uncontrollably for hours without holding back, riding out your raw emotions like a child until you could no longer cry anymore. If the worst came to the worst, truly the worst, then all the anxiety, rage, grief, and fear would be at an end. You would rejoin the eternity of silence from which life is only a brief interruption, and you would be at last, as the prayers so impeccably put it, be at peace.

When you contemplate these possibilities, perhaps whatever it is you are worried about might not so bad after all, even when the worst comes to the worst.

www.ingramcontent.com/pod-product-compliance
Lightning Source LLC
Chambersburg PA
CBHW071240070526
44583CB00017B/2259